PIANO · VOCAL · GUITAR

100 Christmas Carols

ISBN 978-0-634-04756-5

HAL•LEONARD®
CORPORATION

7777 W. BLUEMOUND RD. P.O. BOX 13819 MILWAUKEE, WI 53213

In Australia Contact:
Hal Leonard Australia Pty. Ltd.
22 Taunton Drive P.O. Box 5130
Cheltenham East, 3192 Victoria, Australia
Email: ausadmin@halleonard.com

Visit Hal Leonard Online at
www.halleonard.com

contents

ANGELS FROM HEAVEN

Traditional Hungarian

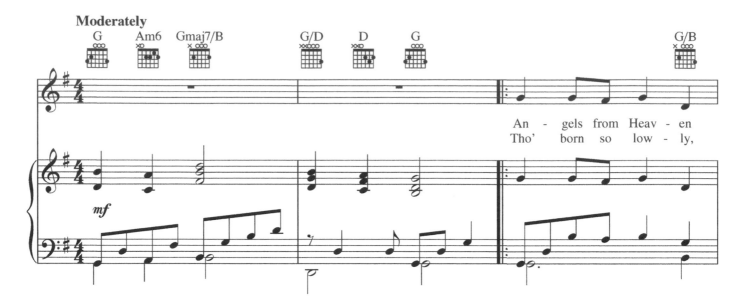

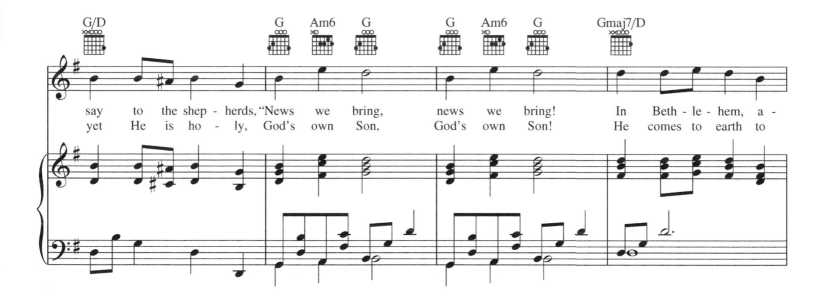

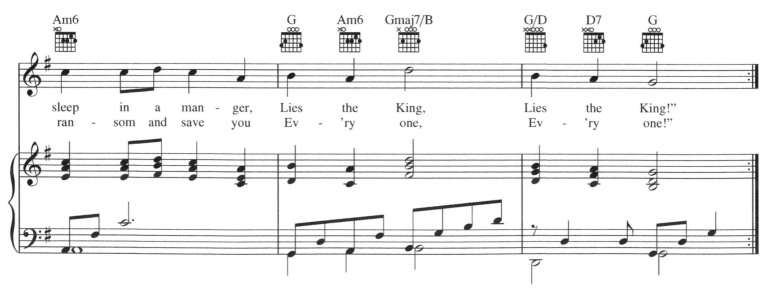

AS EACH HAPPY CHRISTMAS

Traditional

ANGELS FROM THE REALMS OF GLORY

Words by JAMES MONTGOMERY
Music by HENRY T. SMART

Joyfully

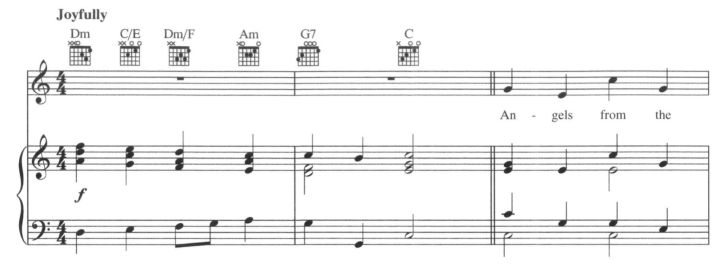

An - gels from the

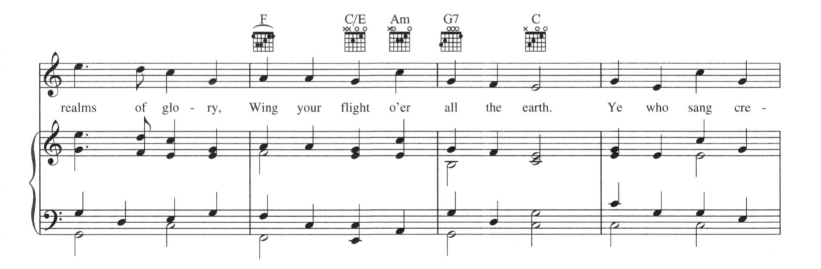

realms of glo - ry, Wing your flight o'er all the earth. Ye who sang cre -

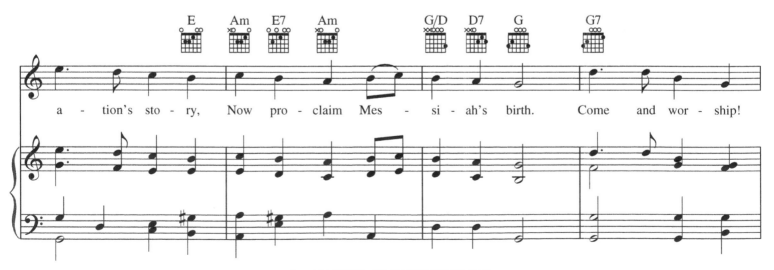

a - tion's sto - ry, Now pro - claim Mes - si - ah's birth. Come and wor - ship!

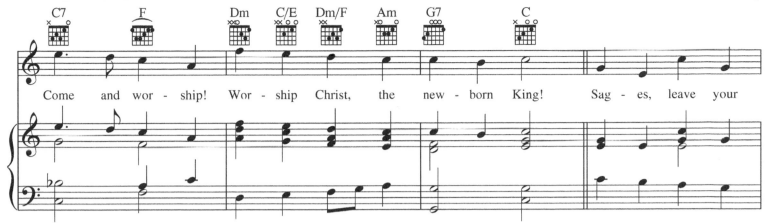

Come and wor - ship! Wor - ship Christ, the new - born King! Sag - es, leave your

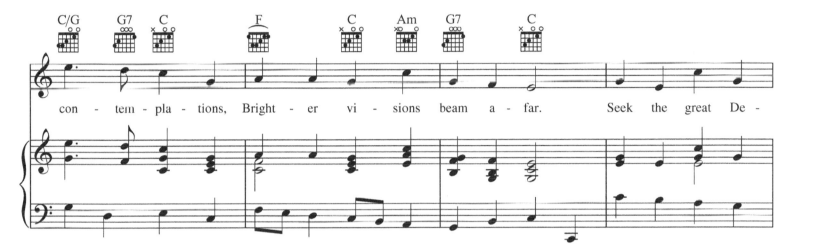

con - tem - pla - tions, Bright - er vi - sions beam a - far. Seek the great De -

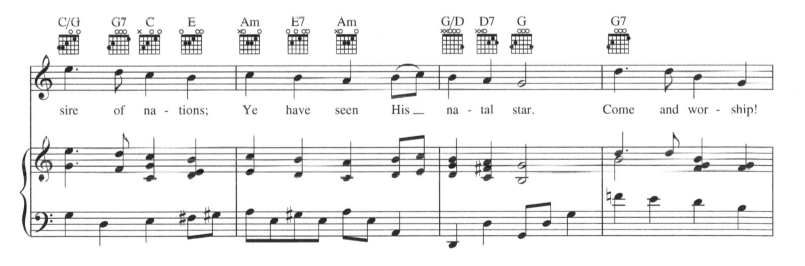

sire of na - tions; Ye have seen His __ na - tal star. Come and wor - ship!

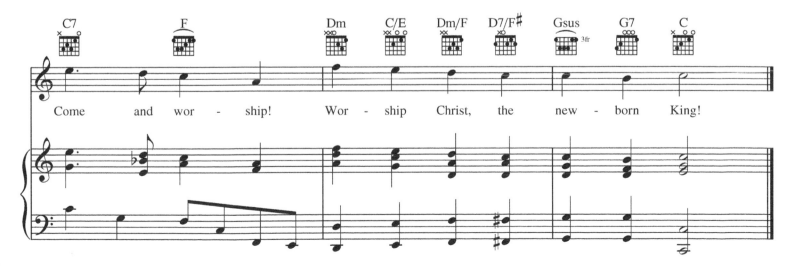

Come and wor - ship! Wor - ship Christ, the new - born King!

ANGELS WE HAVE HEARD ON HIGH

Traditional French Carol
Translated by JAMES CHADWICK

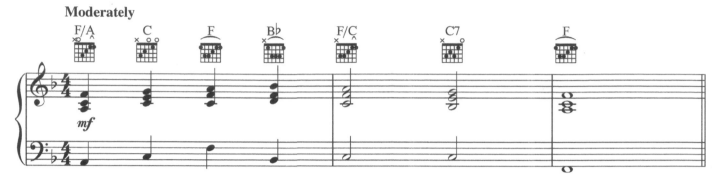

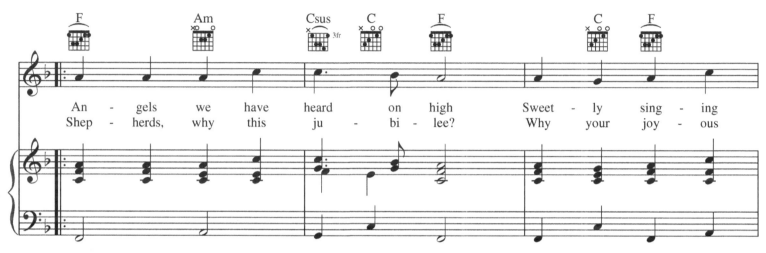

An - gels we have heard on high Sweet - ly sing - ing
Shep - herds, why this heard ju - bi - lee? Why your joy - ous

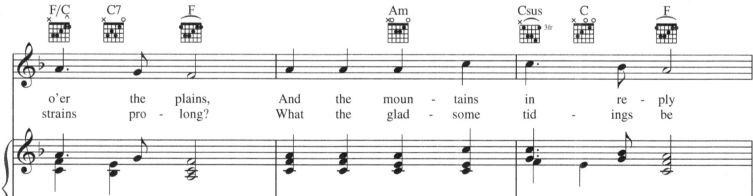

o'er the plains, And the moun - tains in re - ply
strains pro - long? What the glad - some tid - ings be

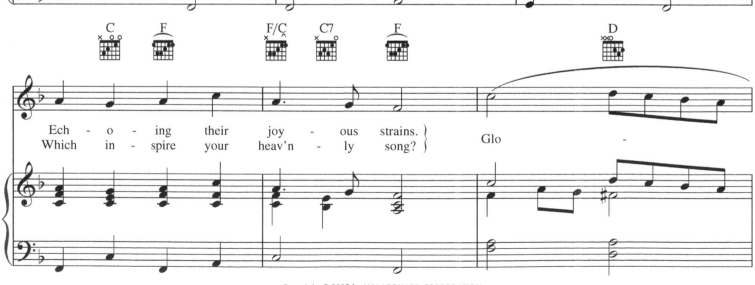

Ech - o - ing their joy - ous strains.
Which in - spire your heav'n - ly song? } Glo -

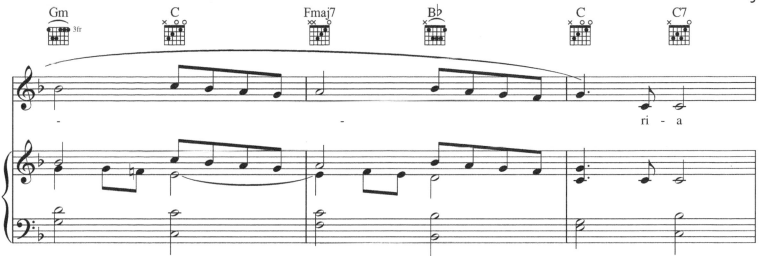

ri - a

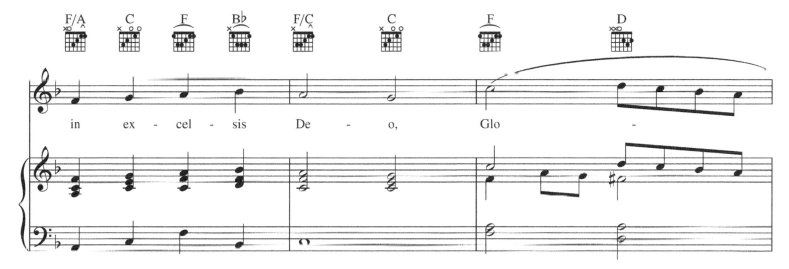

in ex - cel - sis De - o, Glo -

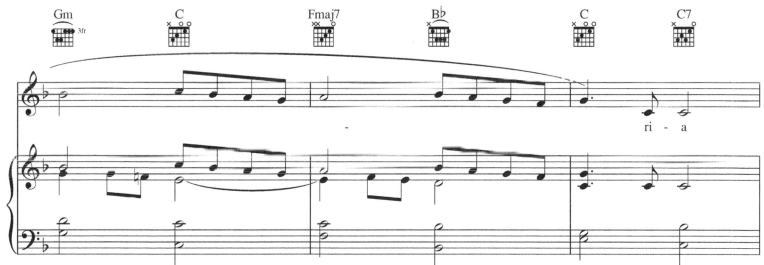

ri - a

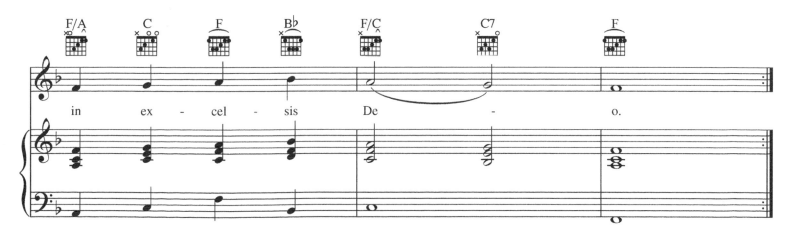

in ex - cel - sis De - o.

AS LATELY WE WATCHED

19th Century Austrian Carol

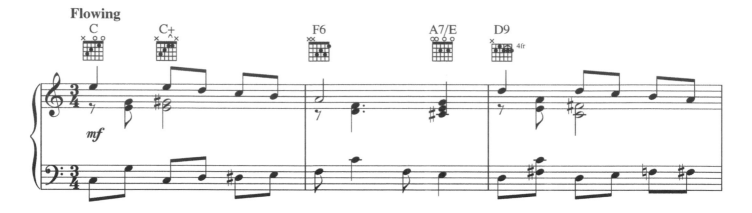

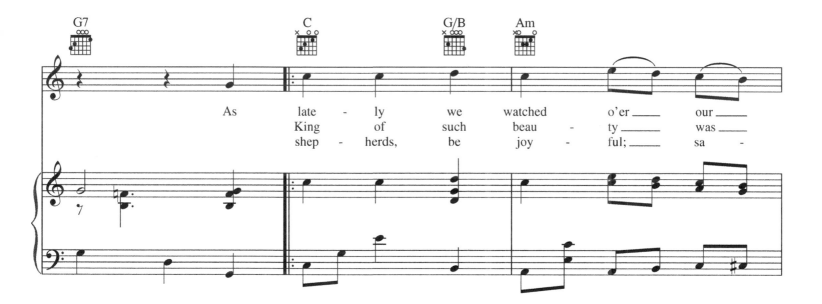

As late - ly we watched o'er___ our
King of such beau - ty___ was___
shep - herds, be joy - ful;___ sa -

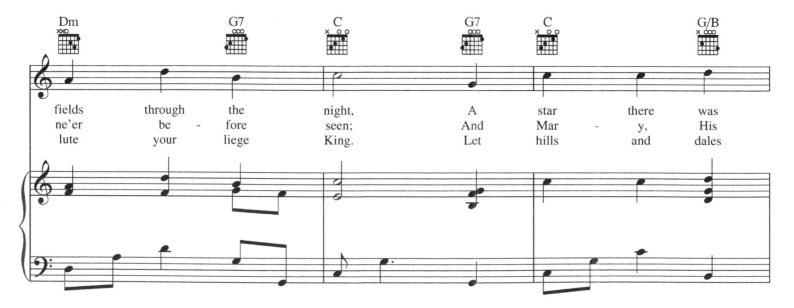

fields through the night, A star there was
ne'er be - fore seen; And Mar - y, His
lute your liege King. Let hills and dales

AS WITH GLADNESS MEN OF OLD

Words by WILLIAM CHATTERTON DIX
Music by CONRAD KOCHER

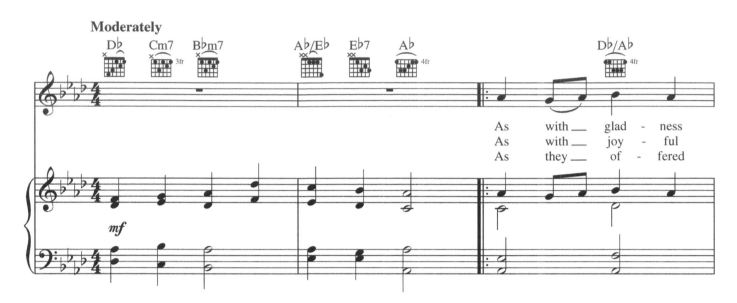

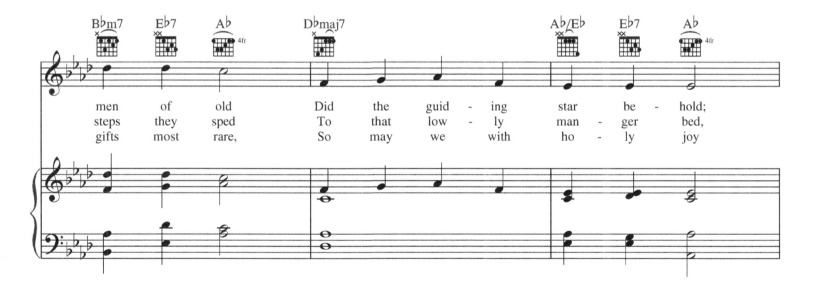

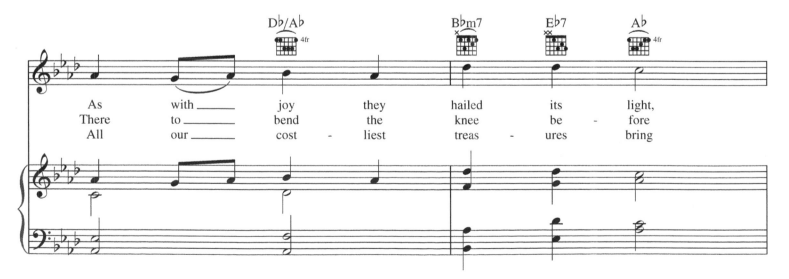

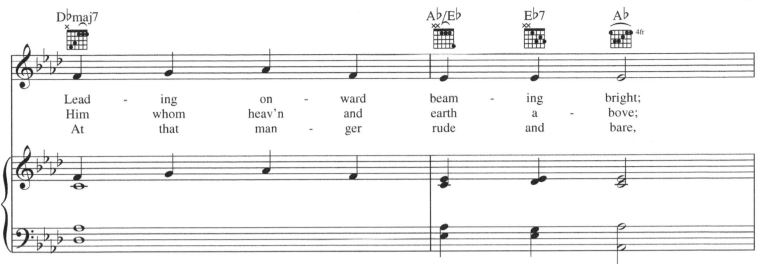

Lead - ing on - ward beam - ing bright;
Him whom heav'n and earth a - bove;
At that man - ger rude and bare,

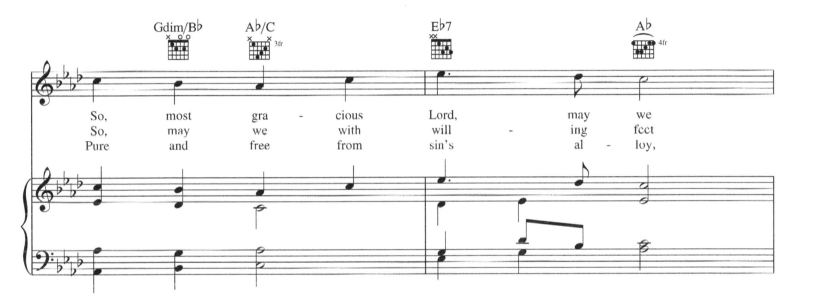

So, most gra - cious Lord, may we
So, may we with will - ing feet
Pure and free from sin's al - loy,

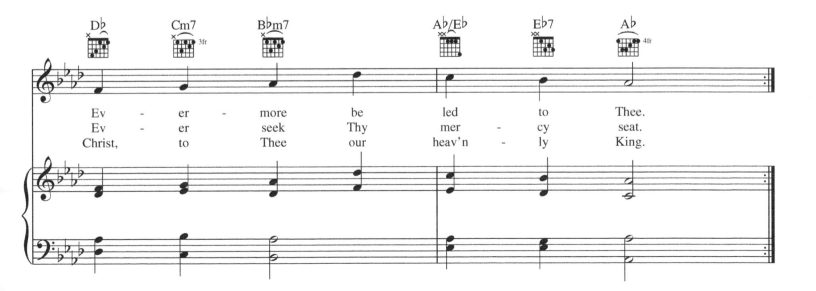

Ev - er - more be led to Thee.
Ev - er seek Thy mer - cy seat.
Christ, to Thee our heav'n - ly King.

AWAY IN A MANGER

Traditional Text
Words by JOHN T. McFARLAND (v.3)
Music by WILLIAM J. KIRKPATRICK

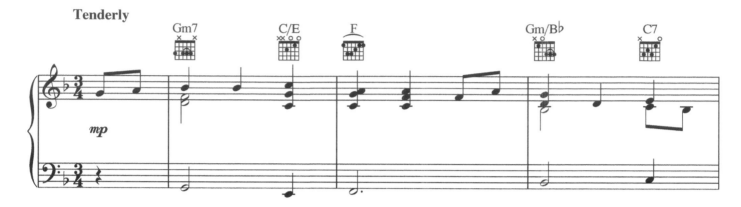

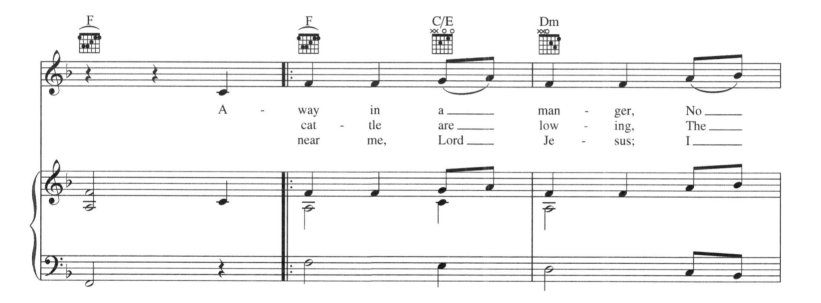

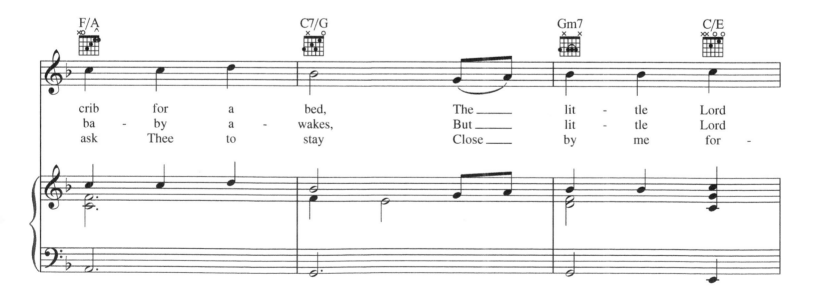

AWAY IN A MANGER

Traditonal Text
Music by JAMES R. MURRAY

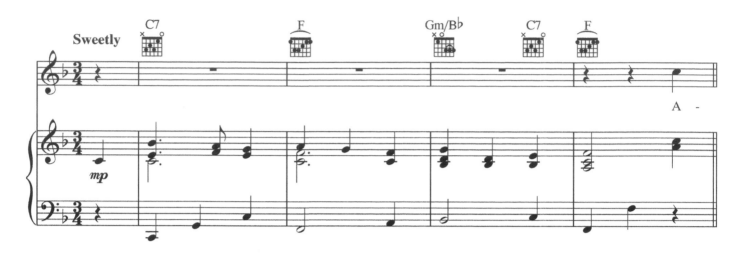

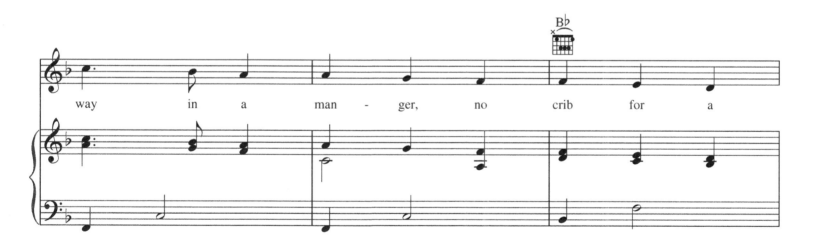

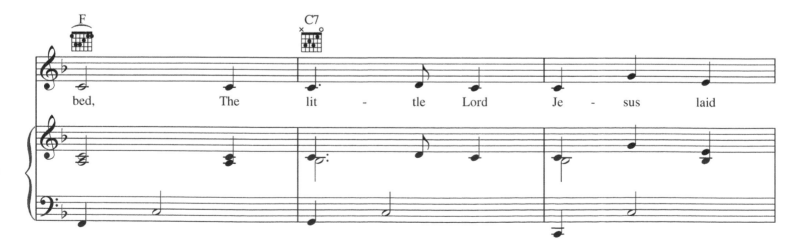

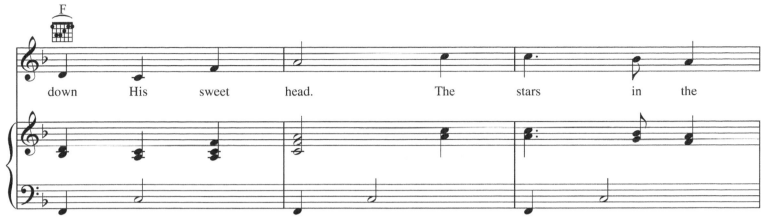

down His sweet head. The stars in the

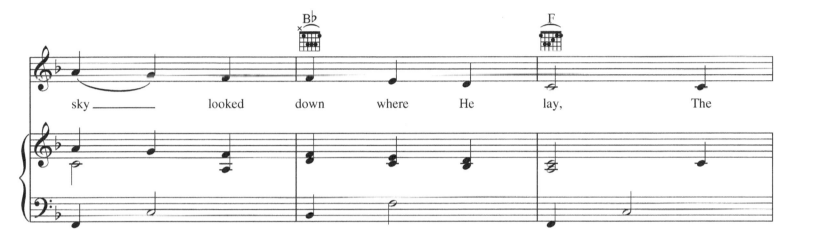

sky _____ looked down where He lay, The

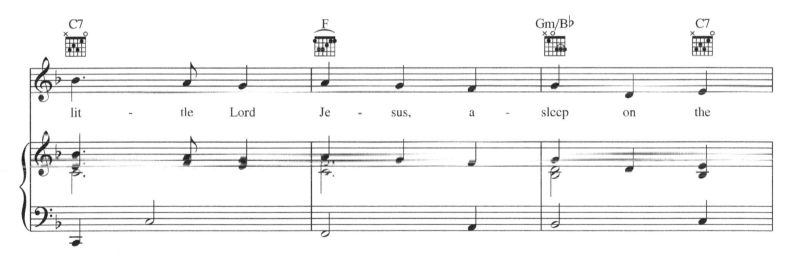

lit - tle Lord Je - sus, a - sleep on the

hay. The cat - tle are low - ing, the ba - by a -

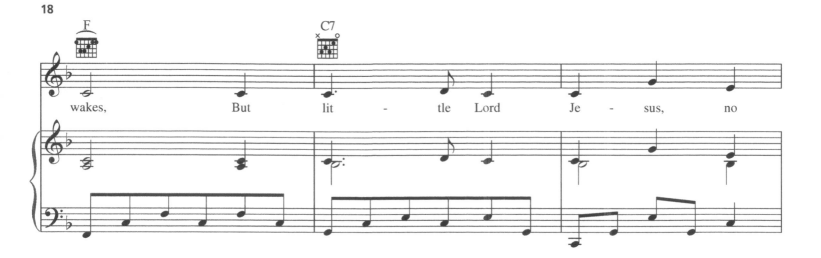

wakes, But lit - tle Lord Je - sus, no

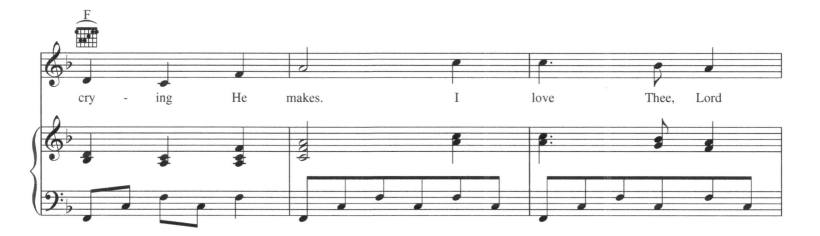

cry - ing He makes. I love Thee, Lord

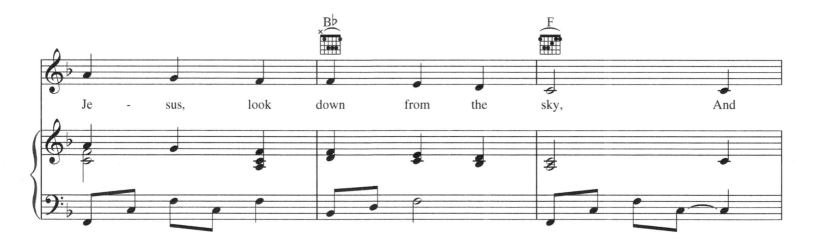

Je - sus, look down from the sky, And

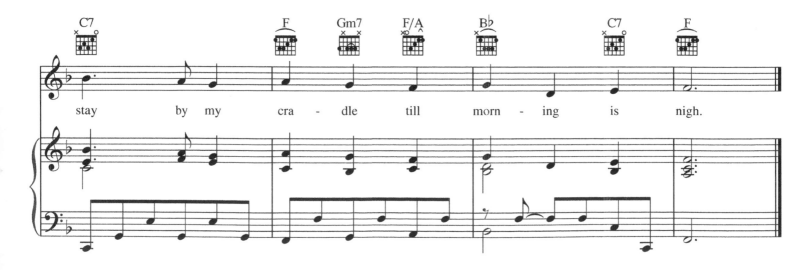

stay by my cra - dle till morn - ing is nigh.

BELLS OVER BETHLEHEM

Traditional Andalucian Carol

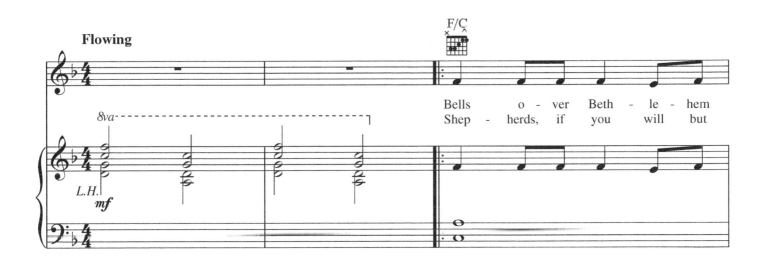

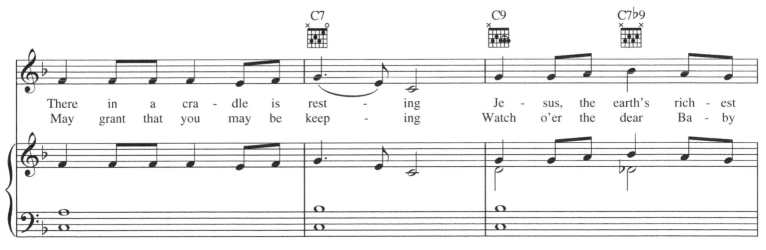

bless - ing!}
sleep - ing.} The bells, the bells of Beth - le -

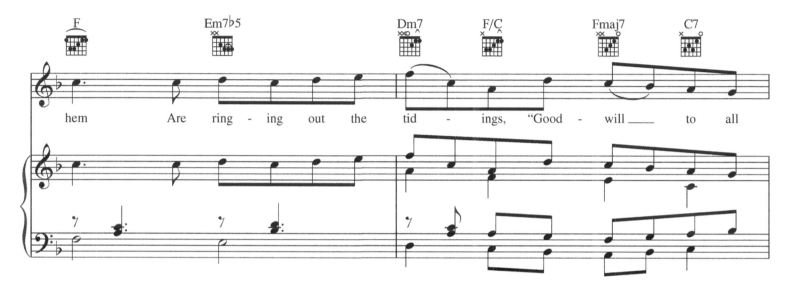

hem Are ring - ing out the tid - ings, "Good - will ___ to all

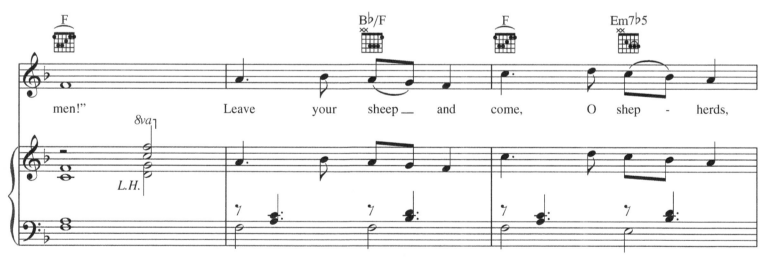

men!" Leave your sheep ___ and come, O shep - herds,

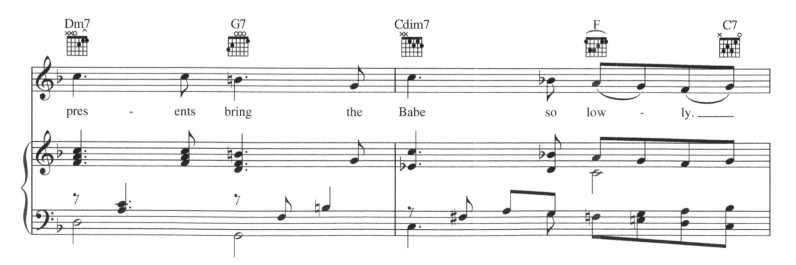

pres - ents bring the Babe so low - ly. ___

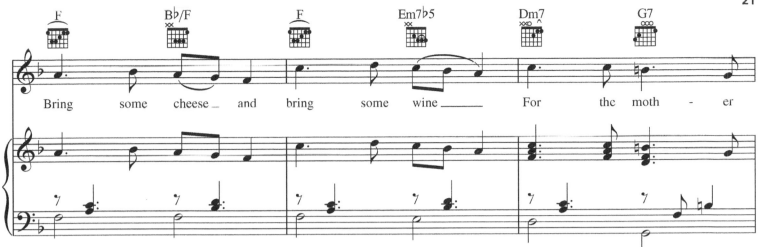

Bring some cheese and bring some wine For the moth - er

Mar - y ho - ly. The bells, the bells of Beth - le -

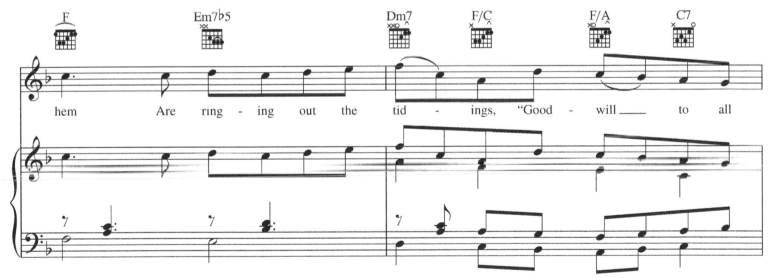

hem Are ring - ing out the tid - ings, "Good - will to all

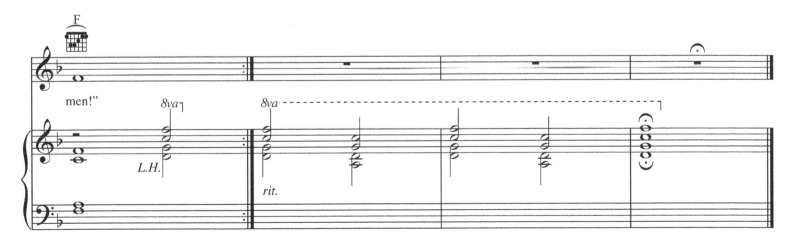

men!"

A BABY IN THE CRADLE

By D.G. CORNER

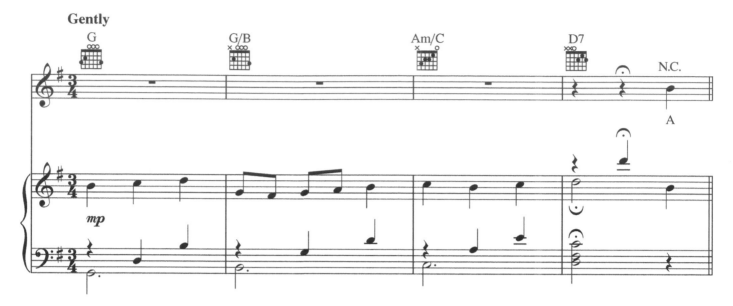

Baby in the cradle, A
Child of whom we're speaking Is
he who rocks the cradle Of
Je-sus dearest Savior, Al-

ti-ny Child so bright; He
Je-sus Christ, the Lord; He
this sweet Child so fine Must
though Thou art so small, With

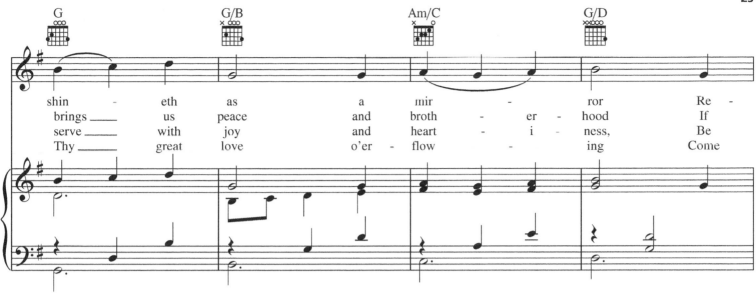

shin - eth as a mir - ror Re-
brings _____ us peace and broth - er - hood If
serve _____ with joy and heart - i - ness, Be
Thy _____ great love o'er - flow - ing Come

flects a no - ble light. _____ This ti - ny
we but heed _____ His Word, _____ Doth Je - sus
hum - ble and _____ be kind, _____ For Mar - y's
flood - ing through _____ my soul, _____ Thou love - ly

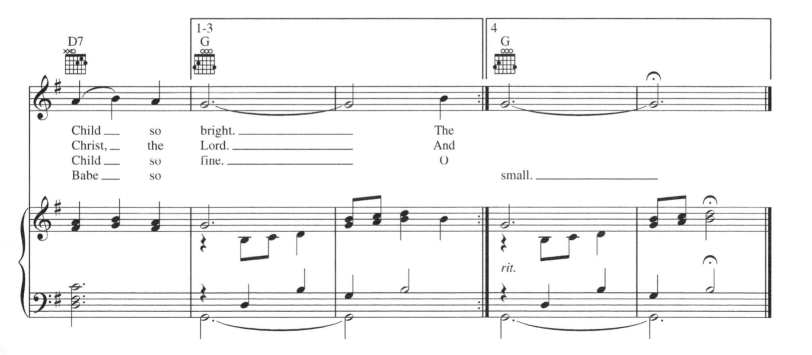

Child _____ so bright. _____ The
Christ, _____ the Lord. _____ And
Child _____ so fine. _____ O
Babe _____ so small. _____

BESIDE THY CRADLE HERE I STAND

Words by PAUL GERHARDT
Translated by REV. J. TROUTBECK
Music from the *Geistliche Gesangbuch*

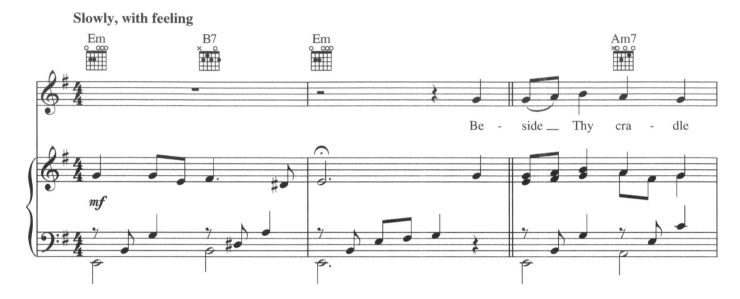

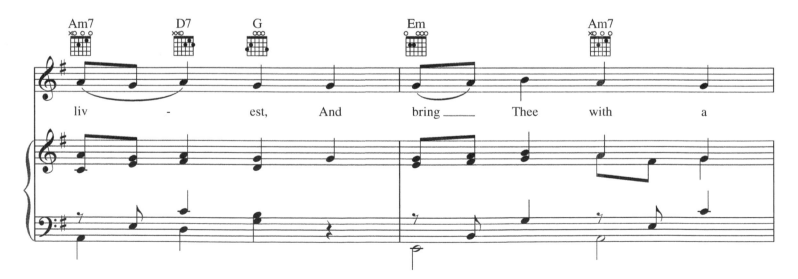

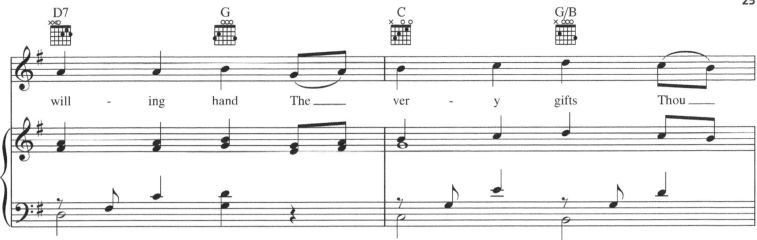

will - ing hand The ___ ver - y gifts Thou ___

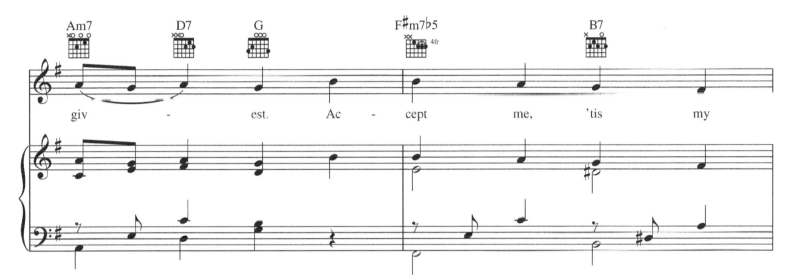

giv - est. Ac - cept me, 'tis my

mind ___ and heart, My soul, my strength, my

ev - 'ry part That ___ Thou from me re - quir - est.

THE BOAR'S HEAD CAROL

Traditional English

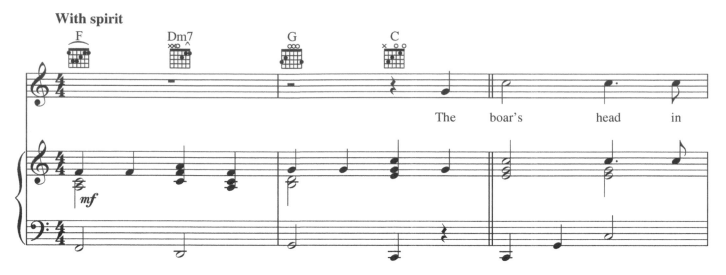

The boar's head in

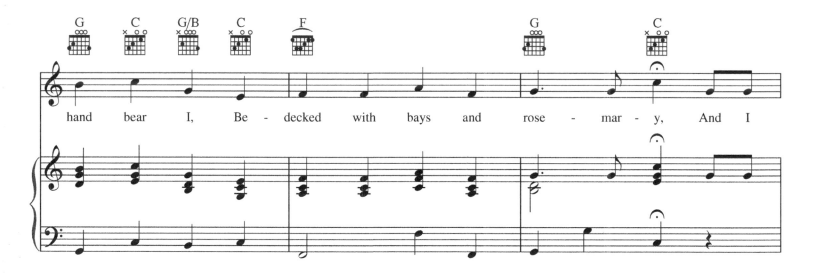

hand bear I, Be - decked with bays and rose - mar - y, And I

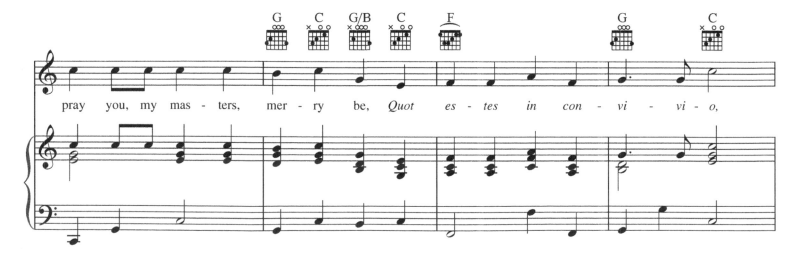

pray you, my mas - ters, mer - ry be, *Quot es - tes in con - vi - vi - o,*

Ca - put a - pri de - fe - ro, Res - dens lau - des Do - mi - no. The

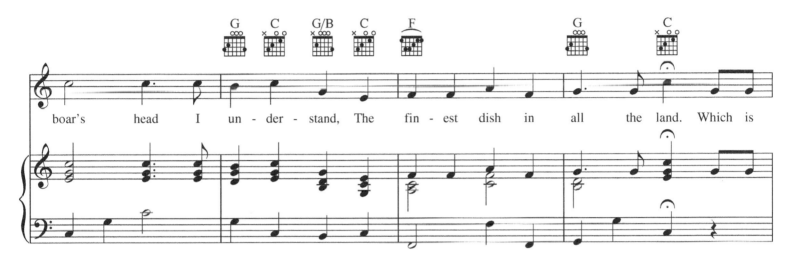

boar's head I un - der - stand, The fin - est dish in all the land. Which is

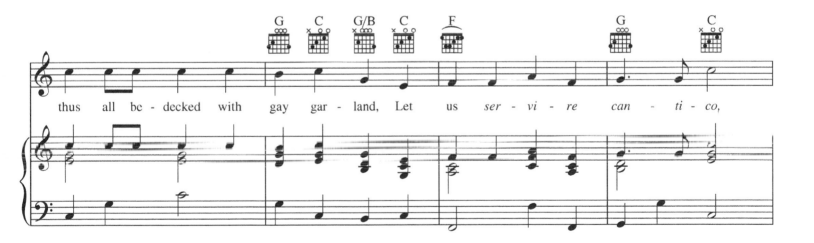

thus all be - decked with gay gar - land, Let us ser - vi - re can - ti - co,

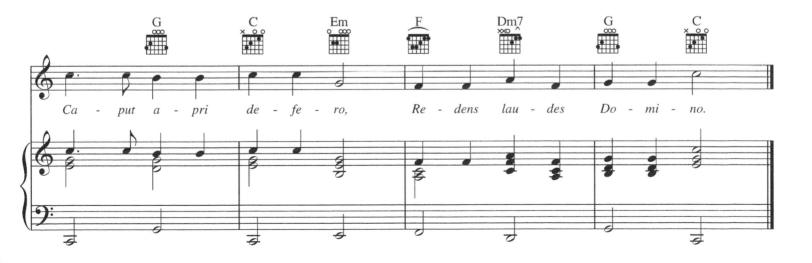

Ca - put a - pri de - fe - ro, Re - dens lau - des Do - mi - no.

A BOY IS BORN IN BETHLEHEM

Traditional

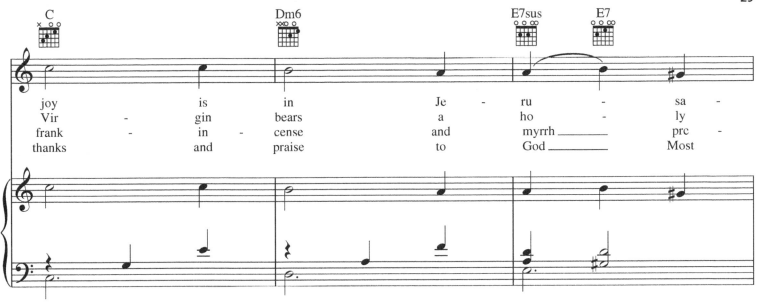

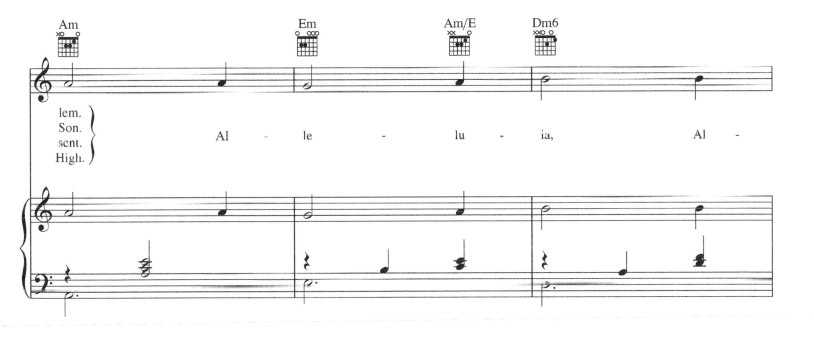

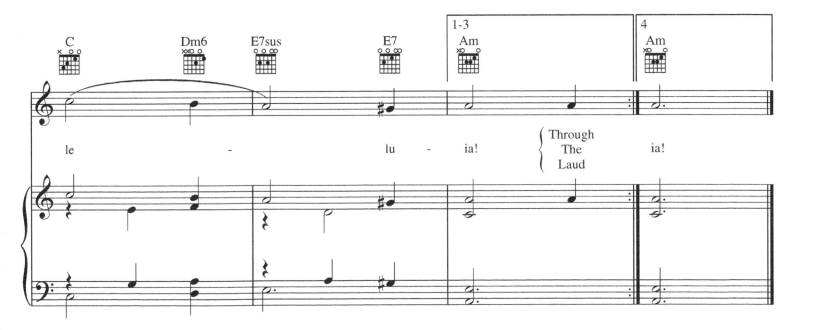

BREAK FORTH, O BEAUTEOUS, HEAVENLY LIGHT

Words by JOHANN RIST
Translated by REV. J. TROUTBECK
Melody by JOHANN SCHOP

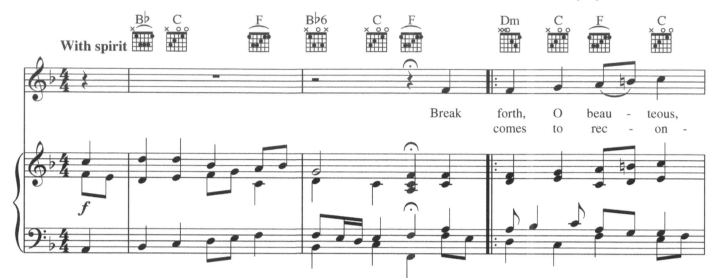

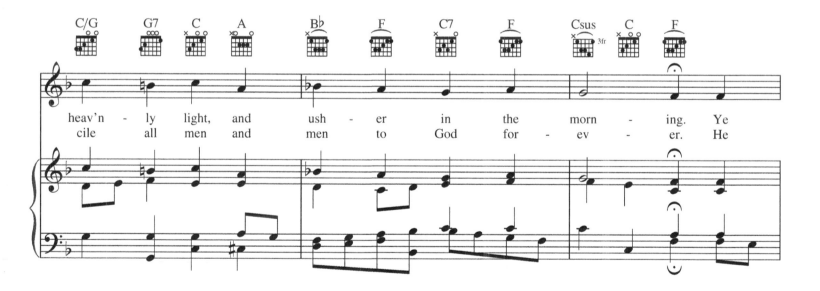

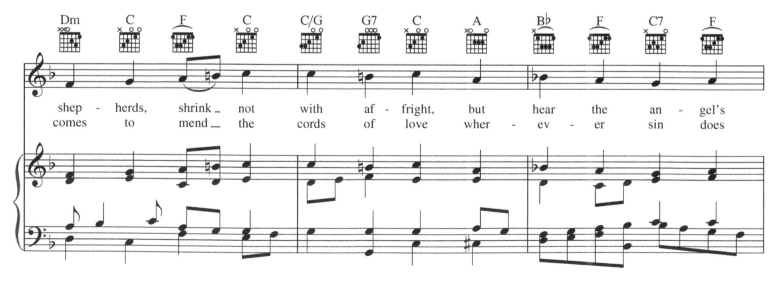

BRING A TORCH, JEANNETTE ISABELLA

17th Century French Provençal Carol

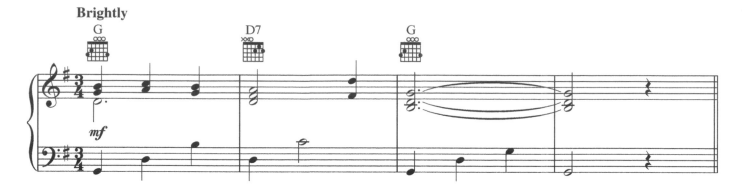

Bring   a   torch,____ Jean - nette   Is - a - bel - la,
Has - ten now,____ good folk of the   vil - lage,

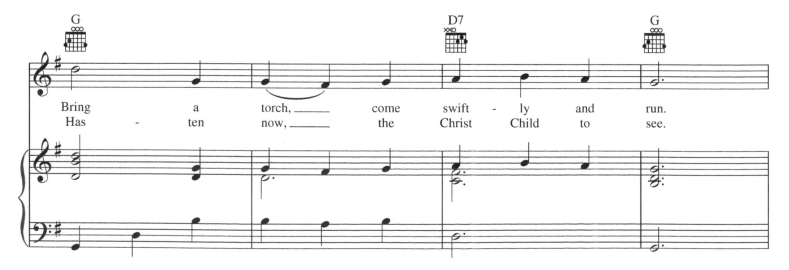

Bring   a   torch,____ come swift - ly and run.
Has - ten now,____ the   Christ - ly Child to see.

Christ is born; tell the folk of the vil - lage.
You will find Him a - sleep in a man - ger.

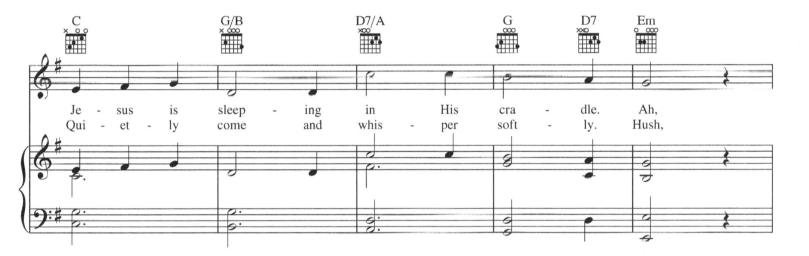

Je - sus is sleep - ing in His cra - dle. Ah,
Qui - et - ly come and whis - per soft - ly. Hush,

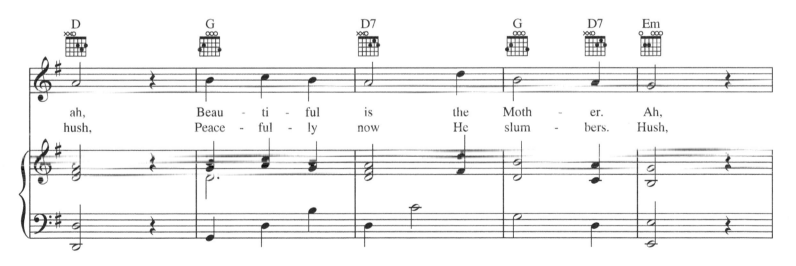

ah, Beau - ti - ful is the Moth - er. Ah,
hush, Peace - ful - ly now He slum - bers. Hush,

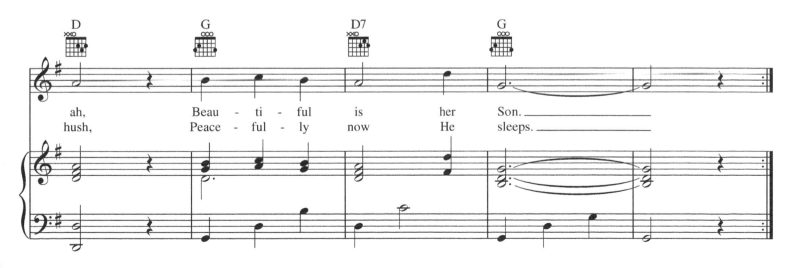

ah, Beau - ti - ful is her Son. _____
hush, Peace - ful - ly now He sleeps. _____

CAROL OF THE BIRDS

Traditional Catalonian Carol

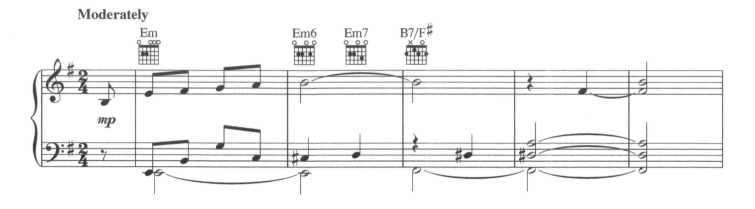

1. Up - on this ho - ly night, When God's great star ap - pears, And
2. night - in - gale is first To bring his song of cheer, And
3., 4. *(See additional verses)*

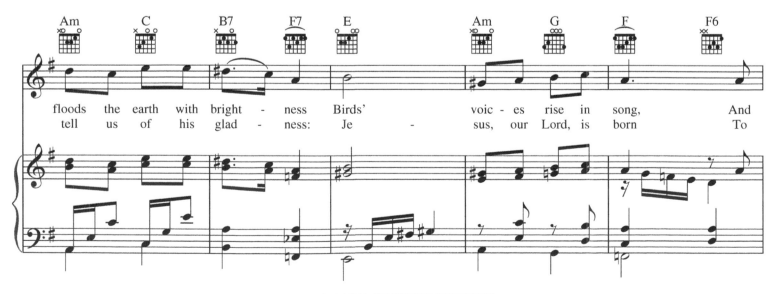

floods the earth with bright - ness Birds' voic - es rise in song, And
tell us of his glad - ness: Je - sus, our Lord, is born To

warb - ling all night long,   Ex - press their glad heart's light - ness.
free us from all sin,   And ban - ish ev - 'ry sad - ness!

Birds' voic - es rise in song, And, warb - ling all night long, Ex -
Je - sus, our Lord is born To free us from all sin, And

press their glad heart's light - ness. The ing."
ban - ish ev - 'ry sad - ness! The

Additional Verses

3. The answ'ring Sparrow cries:
"God comes to earth this day
Amid the angels flying."
Trilling in sweetest tones,
The Finch his Lord now owns:
"To Him be all thanksgiving."
Trilling in sweetest tones,
The Finch his Lord now owns:
"To Him be all thanksgiving."

4. The Partridge adds his note:
"To Bethlehem I'll fly,
Where in the stall He's lying.
There, near the manger blest,
I'll build myself a nest,
And sing my love undying.
There, near the manger blest,
I'll build myself a nest,
And sing my love undying."

A CHILD IS BORN IN BETHLEHEM

14th-Century Latin Text adapted by
NICOLAI F.S. GRUNDTVIG
Traditional Danish Melody

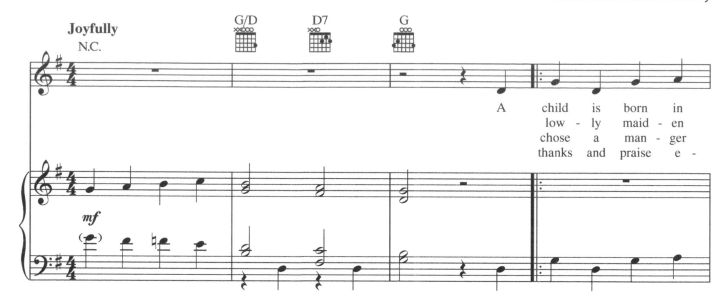

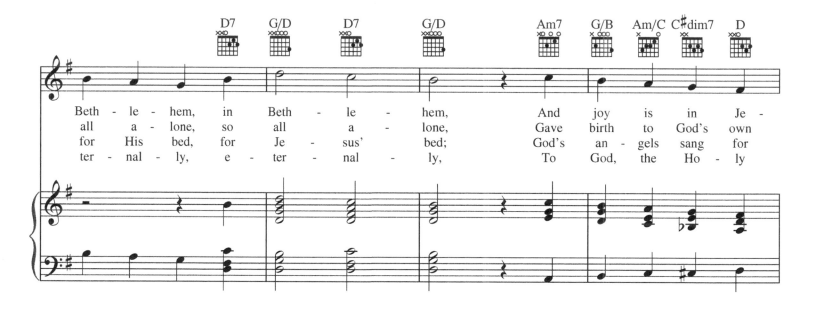

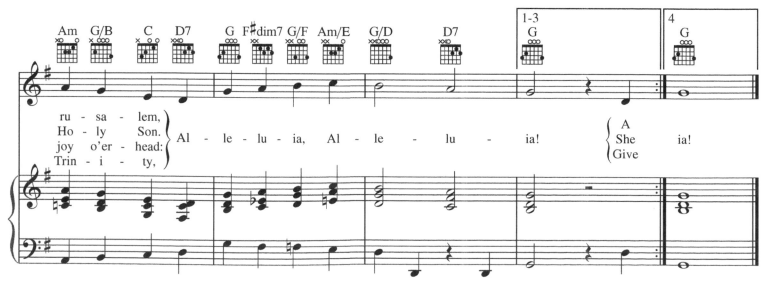

THE CHRISTMAS TREE WITH ITS CANDLES GLEAMING

Traditional Czech Text
Traditional Bohemian-Czech Tune

Like a lullaby

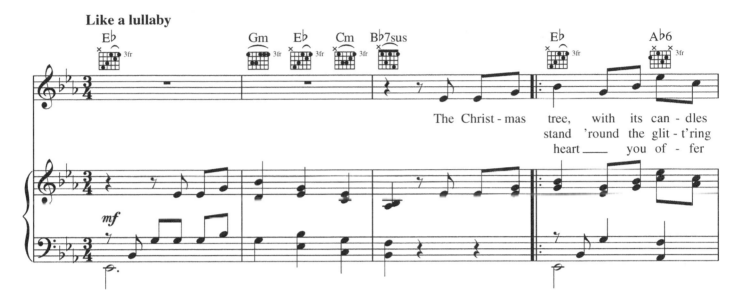

The Christ-mas tree, with its can-dles
stand 'round the glit-t'ring
heart ___ you of-fer

gleam-ing, A glow is kind-ling in all our ___ hearts. It speaks of God's ___ pure love-light
treas-ure; Their eyes are spar-kling, their spir-its ___ bright. O sweet re-mind-er of love's full
bless-ing, For ev-'ry par-ent as well as ___ child. For young and old, ___ your bea-cons

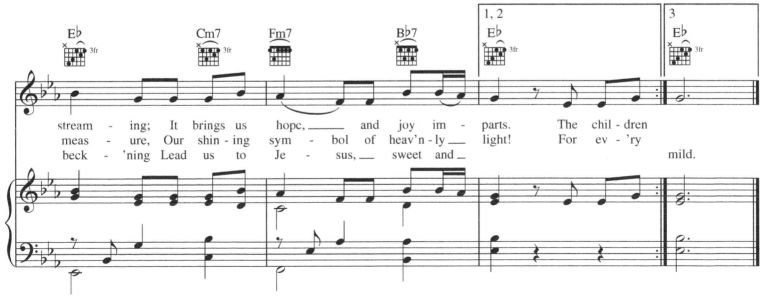

stream-ing; It brings us hope, ___ and joy im-parts. The chil-dren
meas-ure, Our shin-ing sym-bol of heav'n-ly ___ light! For ev-'ry
beck-'ning Lead us to Je-sus, ___ sweet and ___ mild.

CHILD JESUS CAME TO EARTH THIS DAY

Traditional Carol

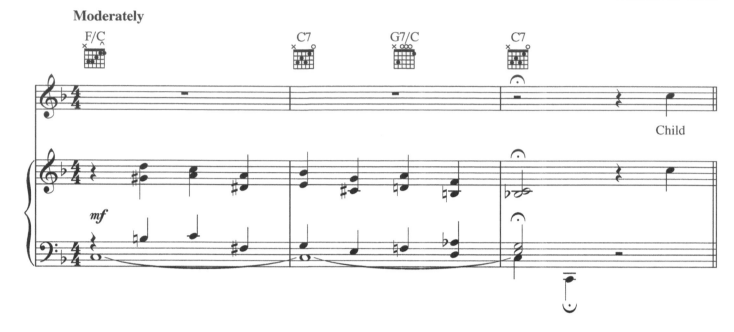

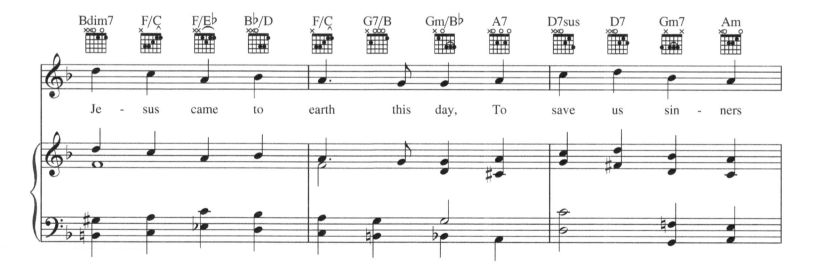

Child Je-sus came to earth this day, To save us sin-ners

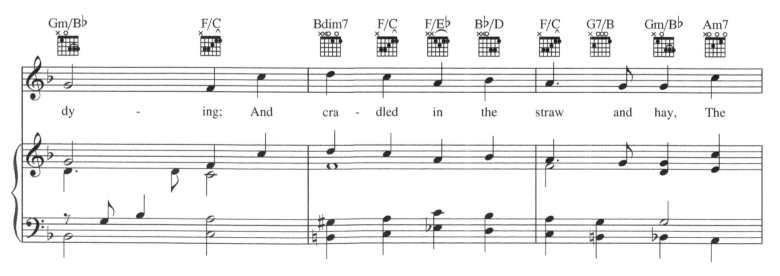

dy-ing; And cra-dled in the straw and hay, The

CHRIST IS BORN THIS EVENING

Traditional

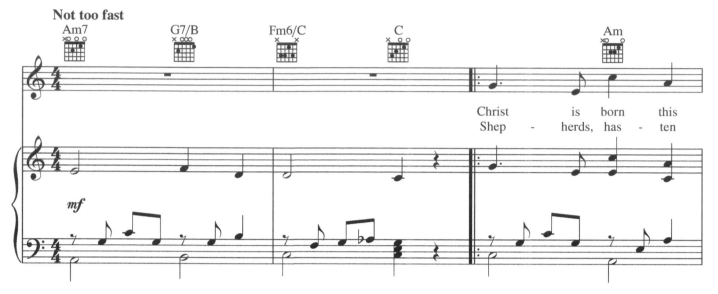

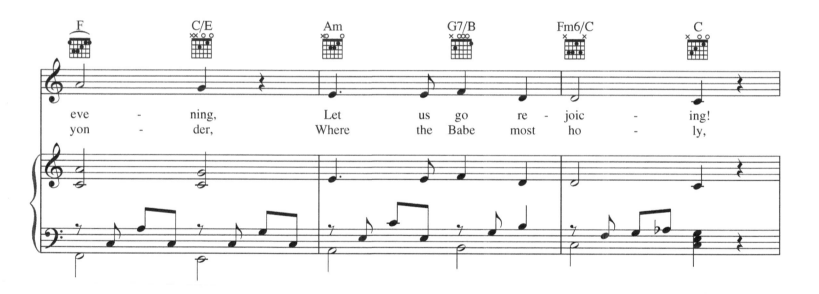

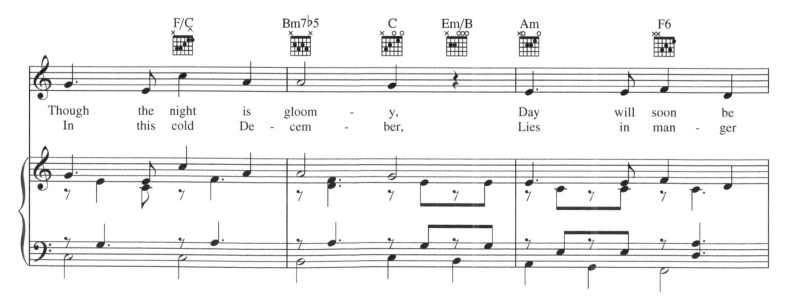

Lyrics:

Christ is born this eve - ning,
Shep - herds, has - ten

eve - ning,   Let   us go re - joic - ing!
yon - der,   Where   us the Babe most ho - ly,

Though   the night   is gloom - y,   Day   will soon be
In   this cold   De - cem - ber,   Lies   in man - ger

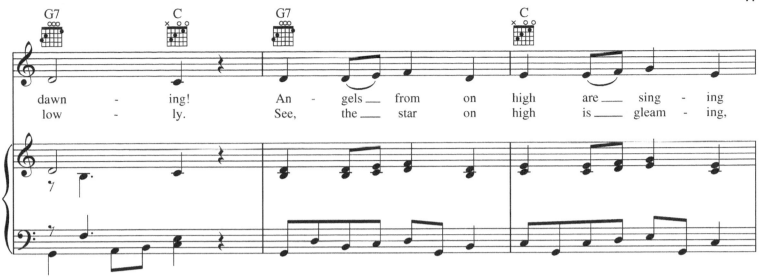

dawn - ing! An - gels ___ from on high are ___ sing - ing
low - ly. See, the ___ star on high is ___ gleam - ing,

To the ___ One who comes from ___ Heav - en:
O'er the ___ love - ly In - fant ___ beam - ing!

Glo - ri - a, glo - ri - a, glo - ri - a,

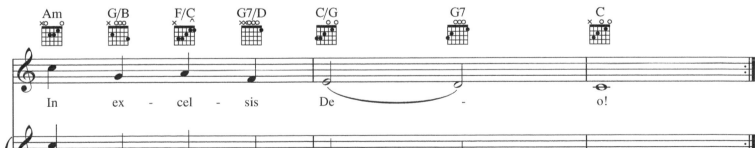

In ex - cel - sis De - o!

CHRIST WAS BORN ON CHRISTMAS DAY

Traditional

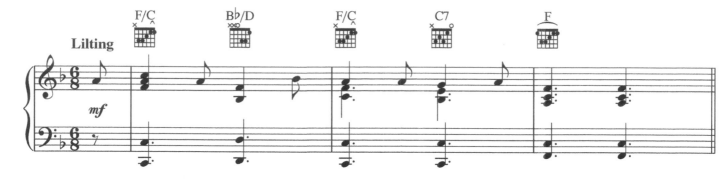

Christ was born on Christ - mas day,

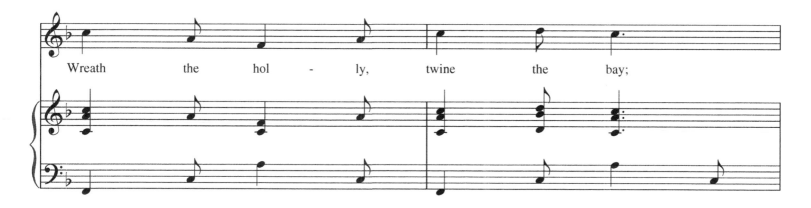

Wreath the hol - ly, twine the bay;

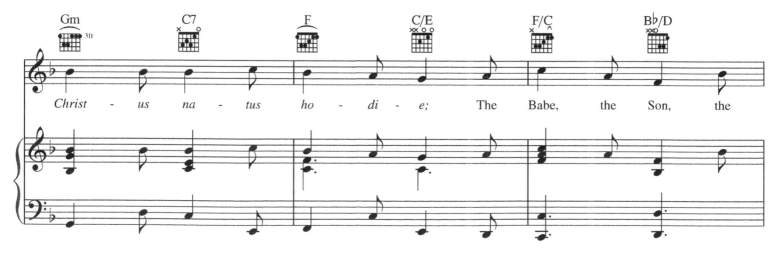

Christ - us na - tus ho - di - e; The Babe, the Son, the

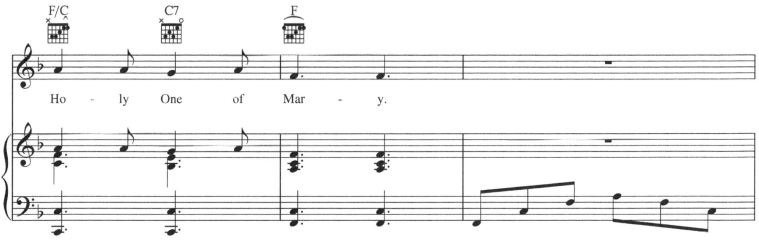

Ho - ly One of Mar - y.

Christ was born on Christ - mas day, Wreath the hol - ly,

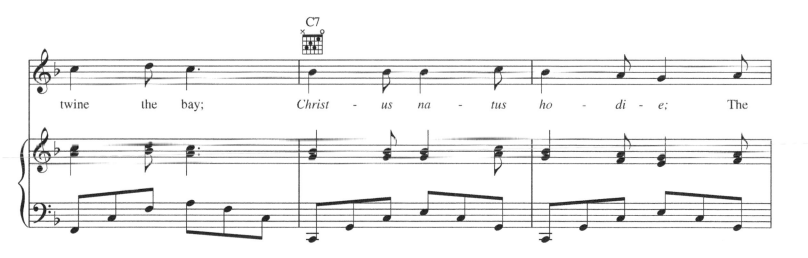

twine the bay; *Christ - us na - tus ho - di - e;* The

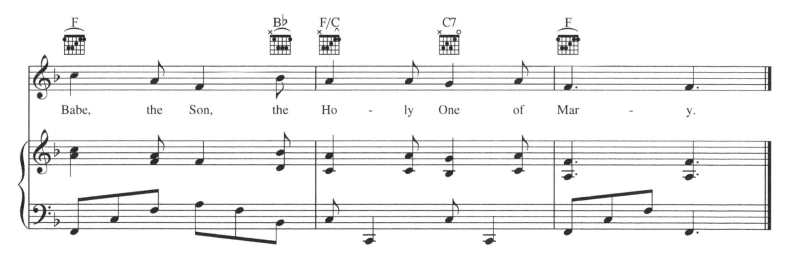

Babe, the Son, the Ho - ly One of Mar - y.

CHRISTIANS, AWAKE! SALUTE THE HAPPY MORN

Traditional

Christ - ians, a - wake, sa - lute the hap - py morn,
Then to the watch - ful shep - herds it was

morn, where - on the Sav - ior of man - kind was
told, who heard th' an - gel - ic her - ald's voice: "Be -

born. Rise to a - dore the mys - ter - y of
hold, I bring good tid - ings of a Sav - ior's

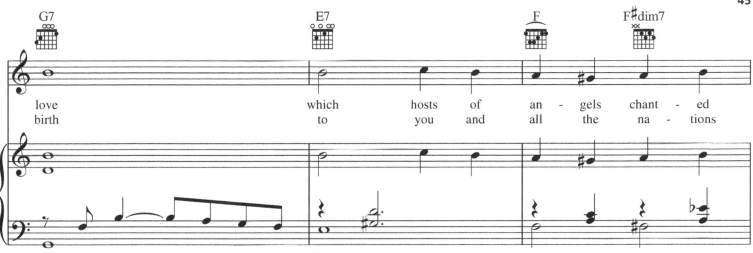

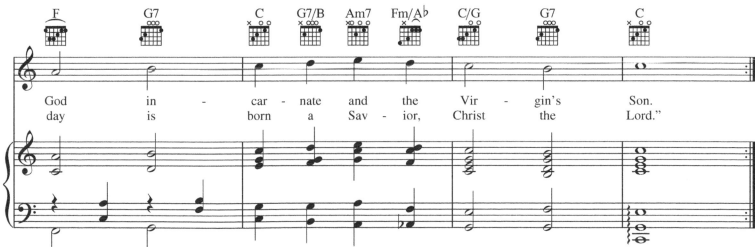

COME, ALL YE SHEPHERDS

Traditional Czech Text
Traditional Moravian Melody

Come, all ye shep-herds, such won-ders en-thrall. Come where the young Child is laid in a stall. This day to us a Sav-ior is giv-en, Whom God on high hath sent down from heav-en; Hal-le-lu-jah!

COME, THOU LONG-EXPECTED JESUS

Words by CHARLES WESLEY
Music by ROWLAND HUGH PRICHARD

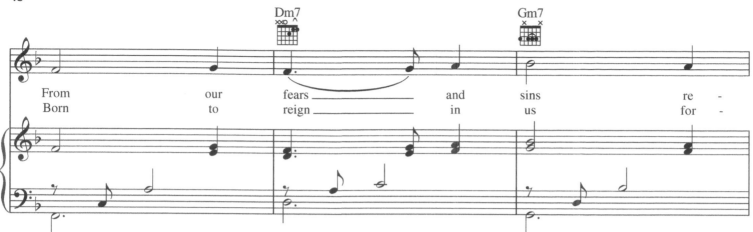

From our fears and sins re-
Born to reign in us for-

lease us; Let us find our
ev - er, Now Thy gra - cious

rest in Thee. Is - rael's
king - dom bring. By Thine

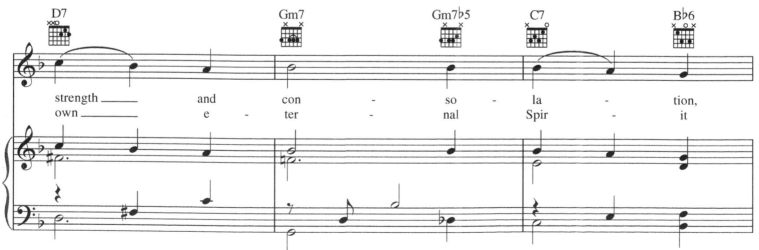

strength and con - so - la - tion,
own e - ter - nal Spir - it

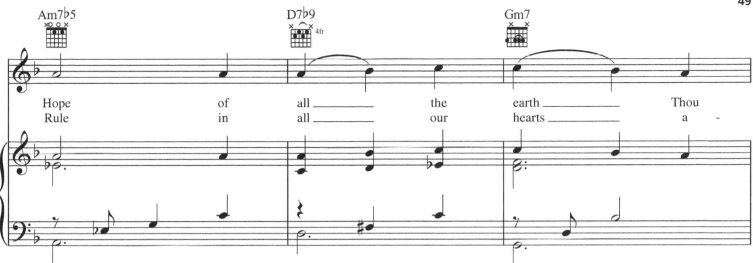

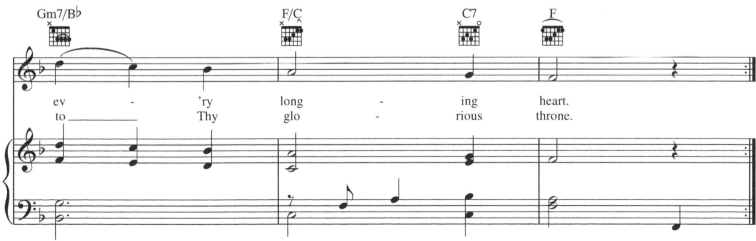

COVENTRY CAROL

Words by ROBERT CROO
Traditional English Melody

Tenderly

1. Lul - lay, thou lit - tle ti - ny child, by by, lul -
2. O sis - ters too, how may we do, for to pre -
3., 4. *(See additional verses)*

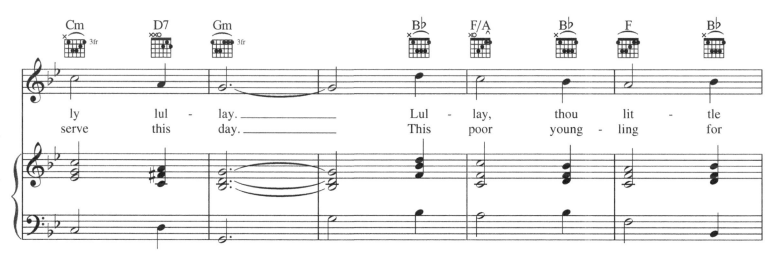

ly lul - lay. _____ Lul - lay, thou lit - tle
serve this day. _____ This poor young - ling for

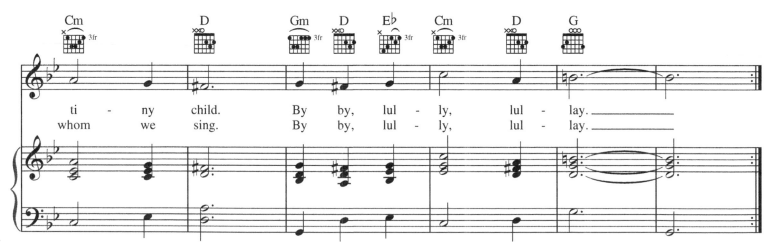

ti - ny child. By by, lul - ly, lul - lay. _____
whom we sing. By by, lul - ly, lul - lay. _____

Additional Verses

3. Herod the king,
In his raging,
Charged he hath this day.
His men of might,
In his own sight,
All young children to slay.

4. That woe is me,
Poor child for thee!
And ever morn and day,
For thy parting
Neither say nor sing
By by, lully lullay!

DANCE OF THE SUGAR PLUM FAIRY
from THE NUTCRACKER

By PYOTR IL'YICH TCHAIKOVSKY

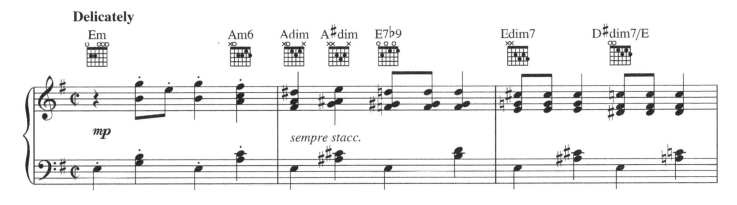

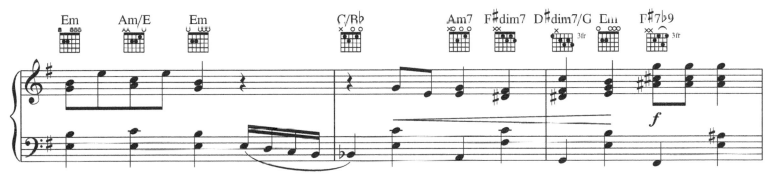

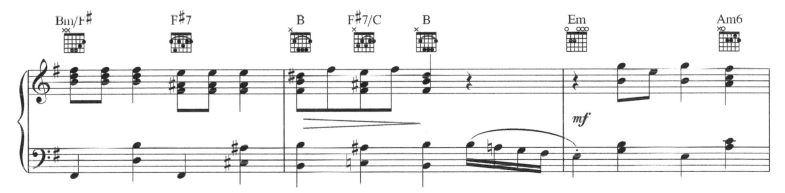

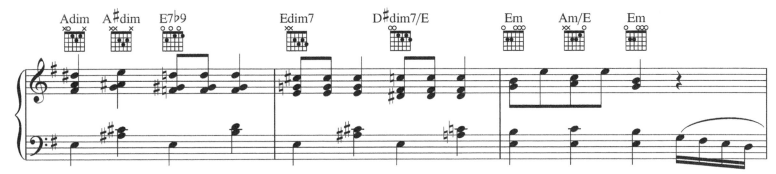

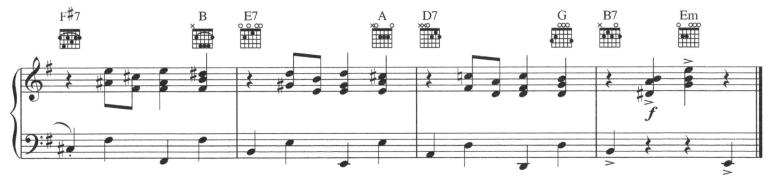

A DAY, BRIGHT DAY OF GLORY

Traditional

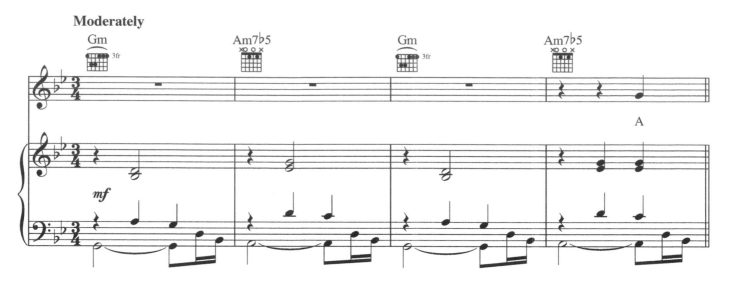

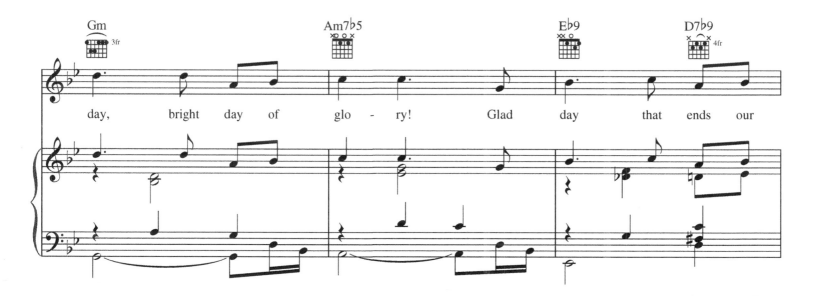

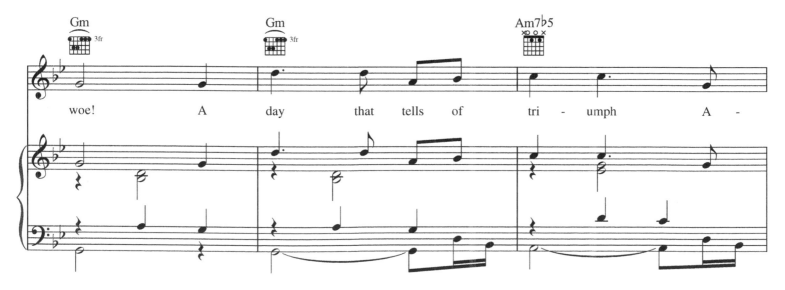

DECK THE HALL

Traditional Welsh Carol

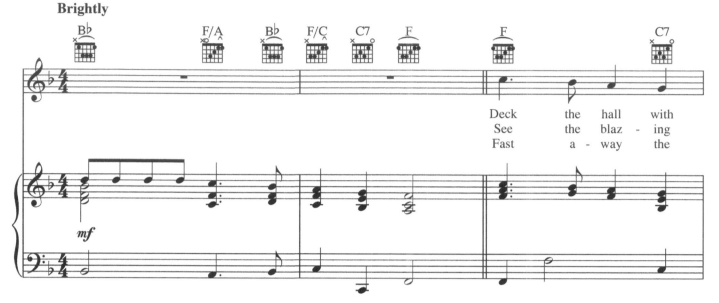

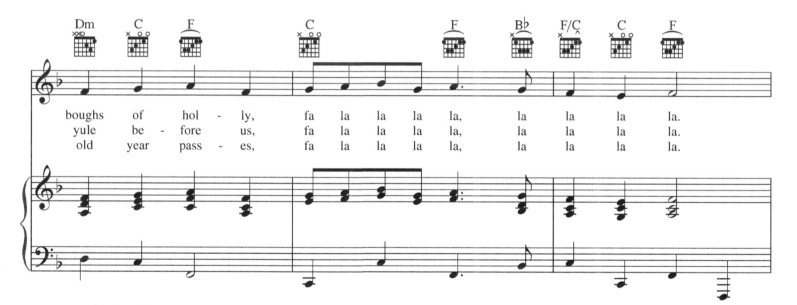

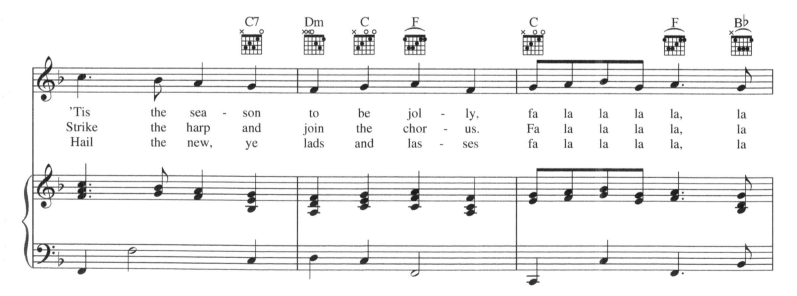

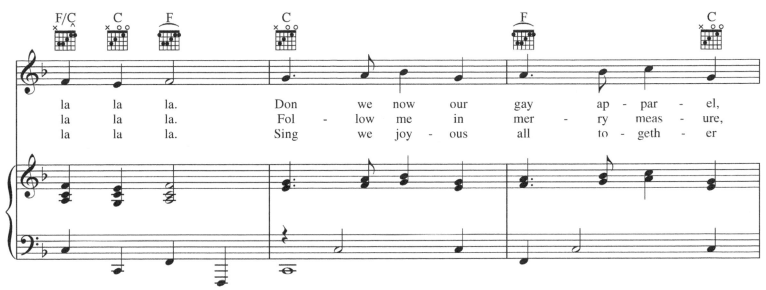

la la la. Don we now our gay ap - par - el,
la la la. Fol - low me in mer - ry meas - ure,
la la la. Sing we joy - ous all to - geth - er

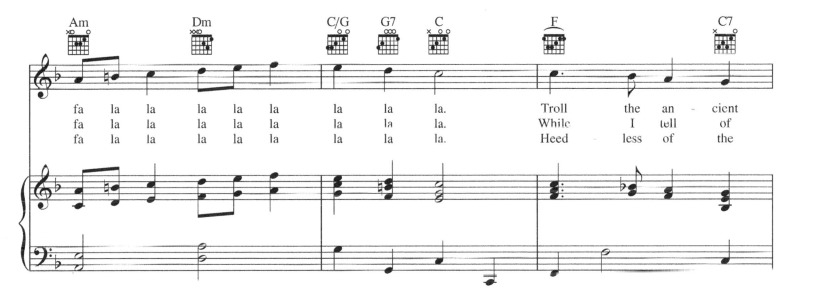

fa la la la la la la la la. Troll the an - cient
fa la la la la la la la la. While I tell of
fa la la la la la la la la. Heed less of the

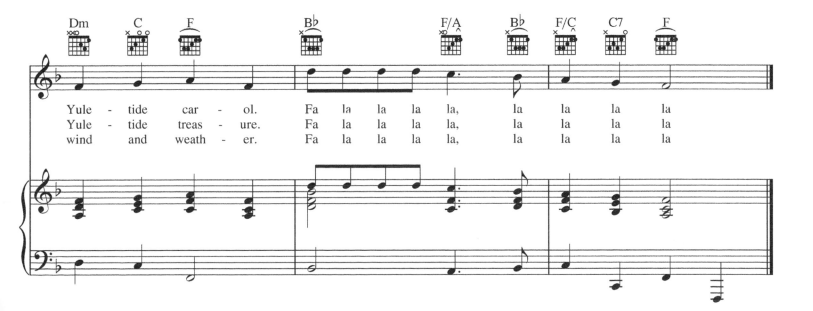

Yule - tide car - ol. Fa la la la la, la la la la
Yule - tide treas - ure. Fa la la la la, la la la la
wind and weath - er. Fa la la la la, la la la la

DING DONG! MERRILY ON HIGH!

French Carol

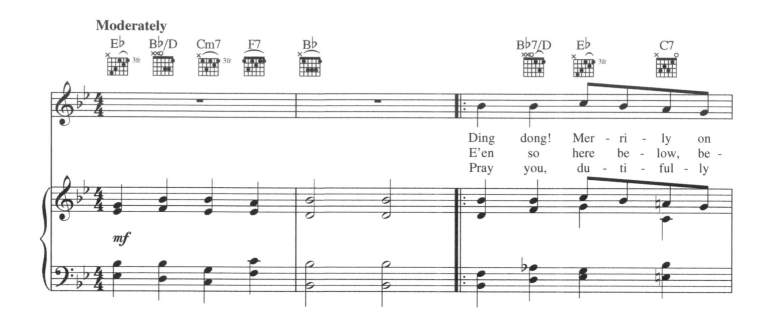

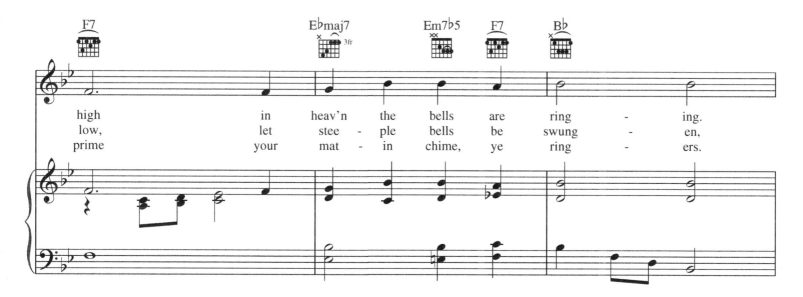

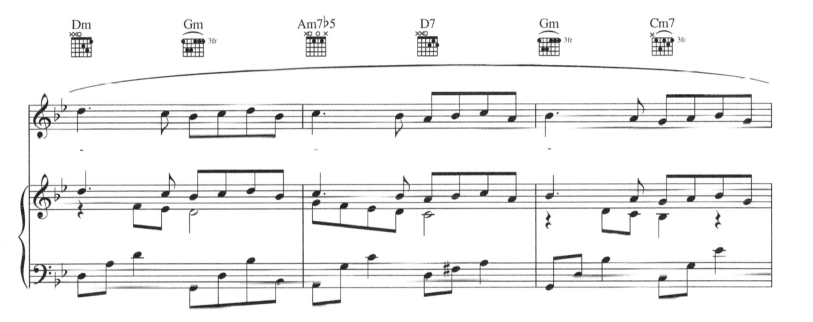

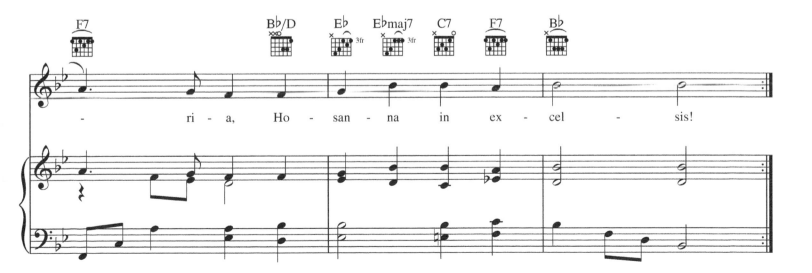

THE FIRST NOËL

17th Century English Carol
Music from W. Sandys' *Christmas Carols*

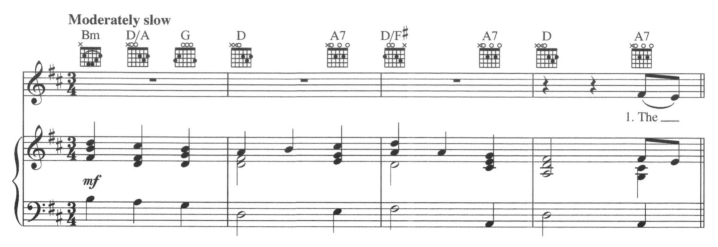

1. The ___

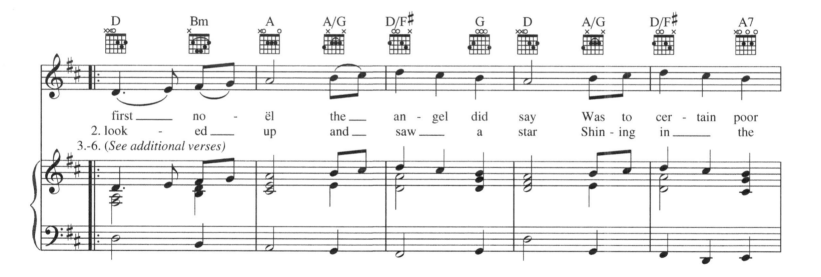

first ___ no-ël the ___ an-gel did say Was to cer-tain poor
2. look - ed ___ up and ___ saw ___ a star Shin-ing in ___ the
3.-6. (*See additional verses*)

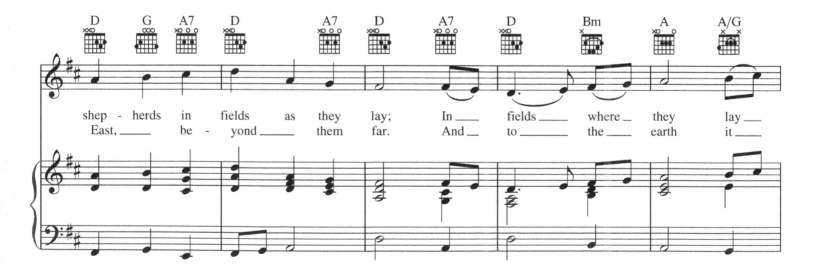

shep-herds in fields as they lay; In ___ fields ___ where ___ they lay ___
East, ___ be - yond ___ them far. And ___ to ___ the ___ earth it ___

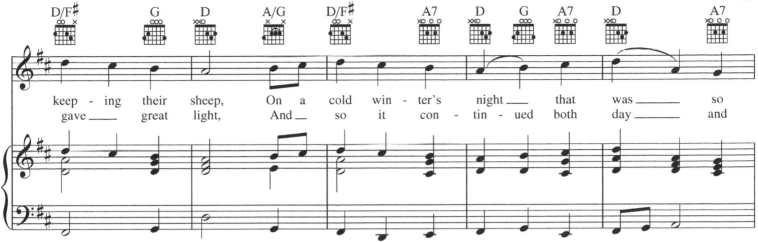

keep - ing their sheep, On a cold win - ter's night ___ that was ___ so
gave ___ great light, And _ so it con - tin - ued both day ___ and

Refrain

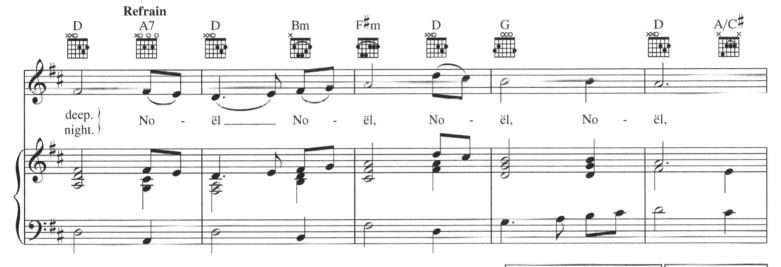

deep. }
night. } No - ël ___ No - ël, No - ël, No - ël,

Born is the King ___ of Is - ra - el. 2. They _ el.
3. And _
4. This _
5. Then _
6. Then _

Additional Verses

3. And by the light of that same star,
   Three wise men came from country far.
   To seek for a King was their intent,
   And to follow the star wherever it went.
   Refrain

4. This star drew nigh to the northwest;
   O'er Bethlehem it took its rest.
   And there it did both stop and stay,
   Right over the place where Jesus lay.
   Refrain

5. Then entered in those wise men three,
   Full rev'rently upon their knee;
   And offered there in His presence,
   Their gold and myrrh and frankincense.
   Refrain

6. Then let us all with one accord
   Sing praises to our heav'nly Lord,
   That hath made heav'n and earth of naught,
   And with His blood mankind hath bought.
   Refrain

THE FRIENDLY BEASTS

Traditional English Carol

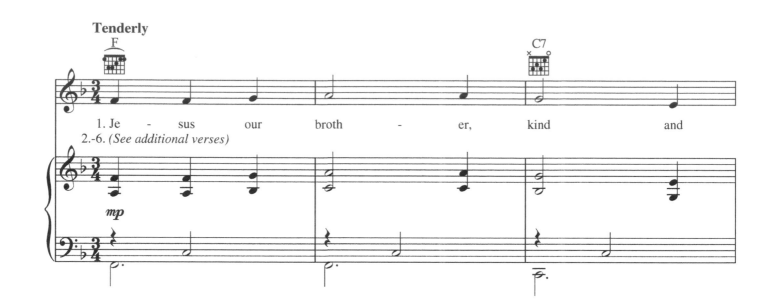

1. Je - sus our broth - er, kind and
2.-6. *(See additional verses)*

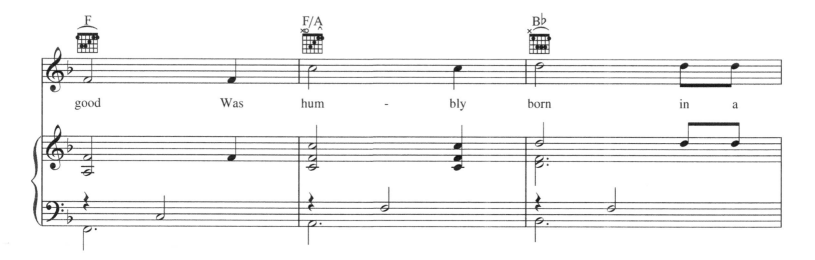

good Was hum - bly born in a

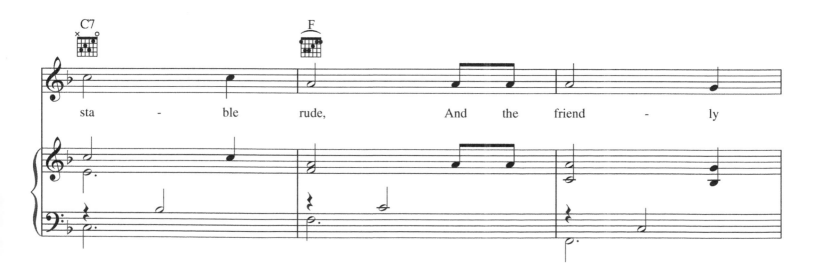

sta - ble rude, And the friend - ly

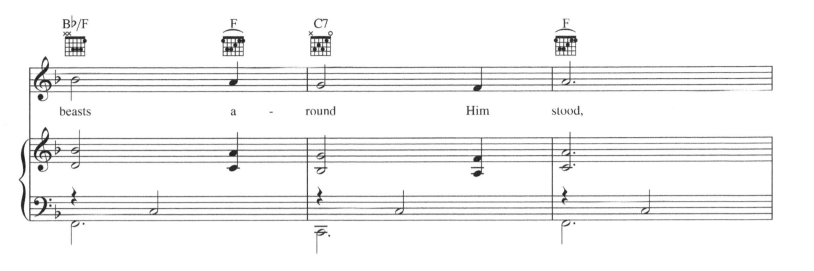

beasts   a - round   Him   stood,

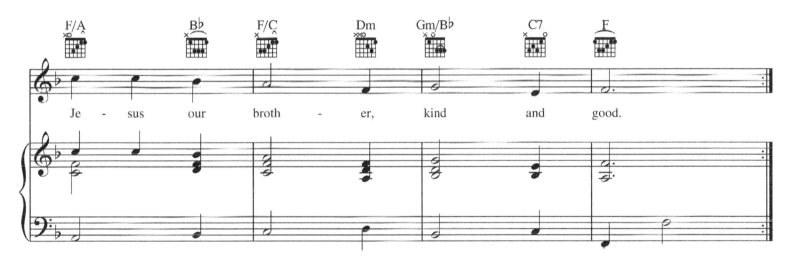

Je - sus   our   broth - er,   kind   and   good.

Additional Verses

2. "I," said the donkey, shaggy and brown,
   "I carried His mother up hill and down;
   I carried her safely to Bethlehem town."
   "I," said the donkey, shaggy and brown.

3. "I," said the cow all white and red,
   "I gave Him my manger for His bed;
   I gave him my hay to pillow His head."
   "I," said the cow all white and red.

4. "I," said the sheep with curly horn,
   "I gave Him my wool for His blanket warm;
   He wore my coat on Christmas morn."
   "I," said the sheep with curly horn.

5. "I," said the dove from the rafters high,
   "I cooed Him to sleep so He would not cry;
   We cooed Him to sleep, my mate and I."
   "I," said the dove from the rafters high.

6. Thus every beast by some good spell,
   In the stable dark was glad to tell
   Of the gift he gave Emmanuel,
   The gift he gave Emmanuel.

FROM HEAVEN ABOVE TO EARTH I COME

Words and Music by
MARTIN LUTHER

FUM, FUM, FUM

Traditional Catalonian Carol

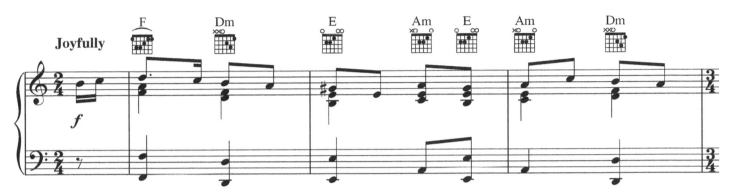

On this joy - ful Christ - mas day sing

Fum, Fum, Fum. On this joy - ful Christ - mas day sing

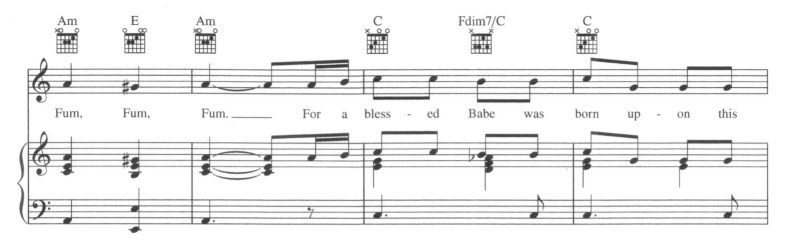

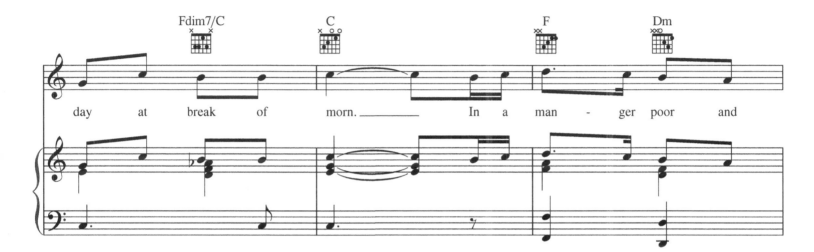

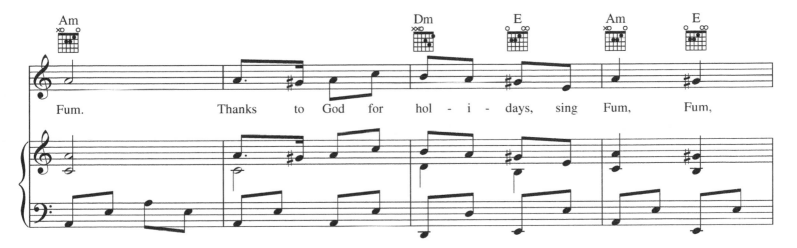

Fum. Thanks to God for hol - i - days, sing Fum, Fum,

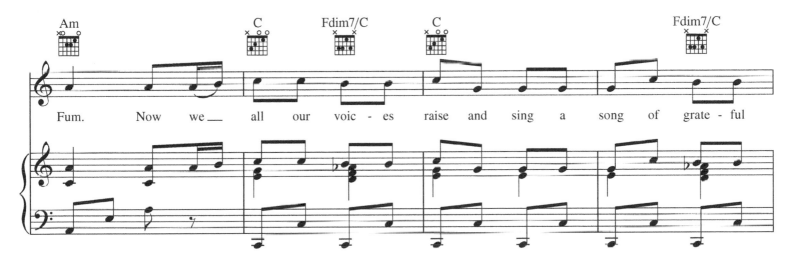

Fum. Now we __ all our voic - es raise and sing a song of grate - ful

praise, __ Cel - e - brate in song and sto - ry all the

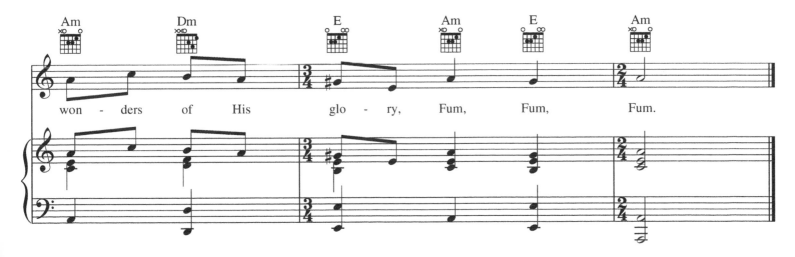

won - ders of His glo - ry, Fum, Fum, Fum.

GO, TELL IT ON THE MOUNTAIN

African-American Spiritual
Verses by JOHN W. WORK, JR.

Moderate Swing

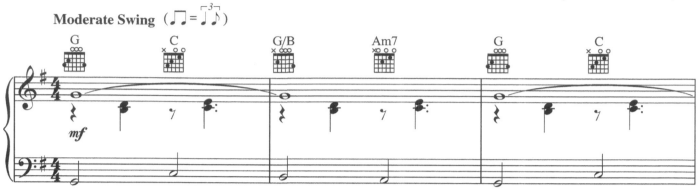

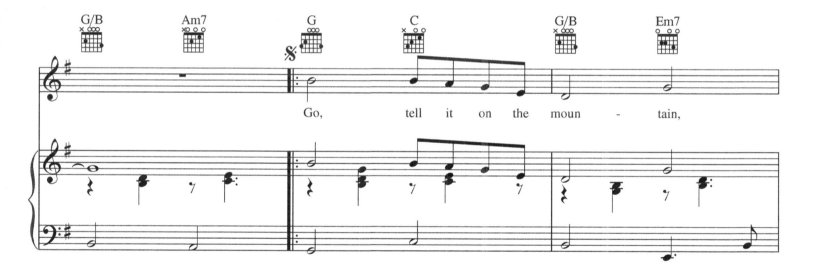

Go, tell it on the moun - tain,

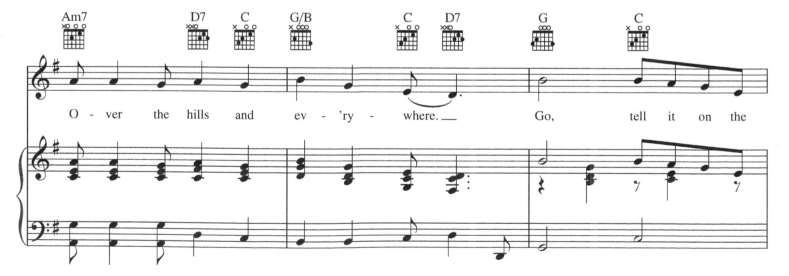

O - ver the hills and ev - 'ry - where. Go, tell it on the

GOD REST YE MERRY, GENTLEMEN

19th Century English Carol

save us all from Sa tan's power when we were gone a-
which His all moth - er Mar - y did we noth - ing take in
that in Beth - le - hem was born the Son of God by

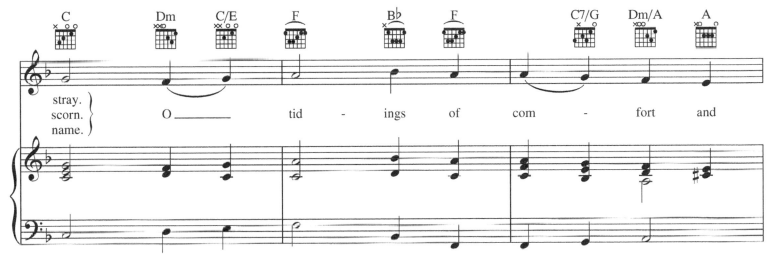

stray.
scorn.
name.

O _____ tid - ings of com - fort and

joy, com - fort and joy; O tid - ings of

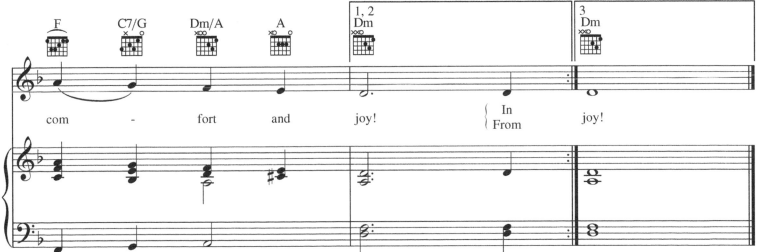

com - fort and joy!

In
From joy!

GOOD CHRISTIAN MEN, REJOICE

14th Century Latin Text
Translated by JOHN MASON NEALE
14th Century German Melody

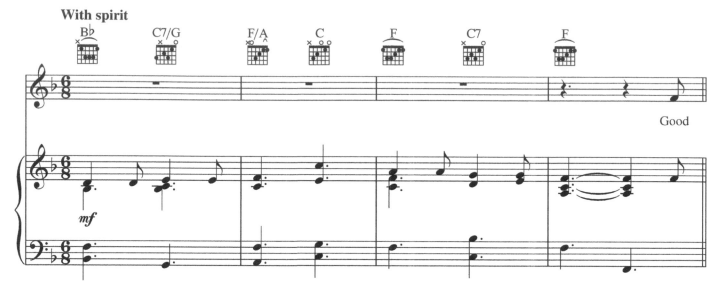

Chris - tian men, re - joice _____ with heart and soul and
Chris - tian men, re - joice _____ with heart and soul and

voice, _____ Give ye heed to what we say:
voice, _____ Now ye hear of end - less bliss;

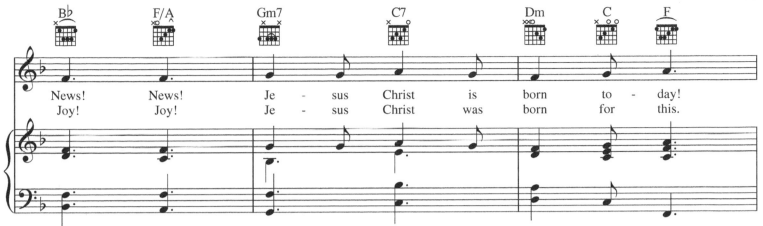

News! News! Je - sus Christ is born to - day!
Joy! Joy! Je - sus Christ was born for this.

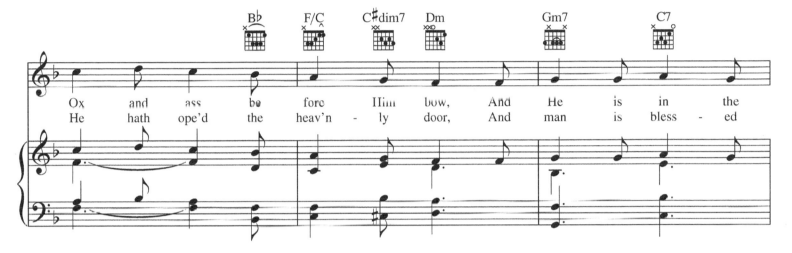

Ox and ass be fore Him bow, And He is in the
He hath ope'd the heav'n - ly door, And And man is bless - ed

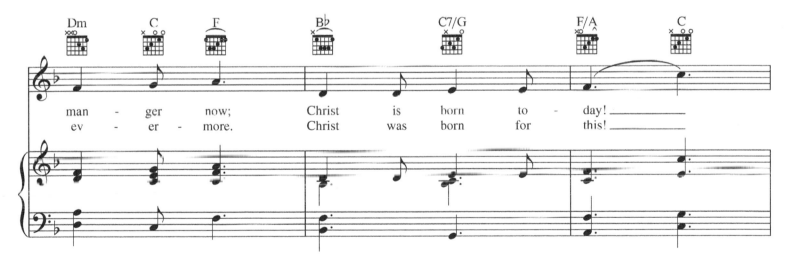

man - ger now; Christ is born to - day! _____
ev - er - more. Christ was born for this! _____

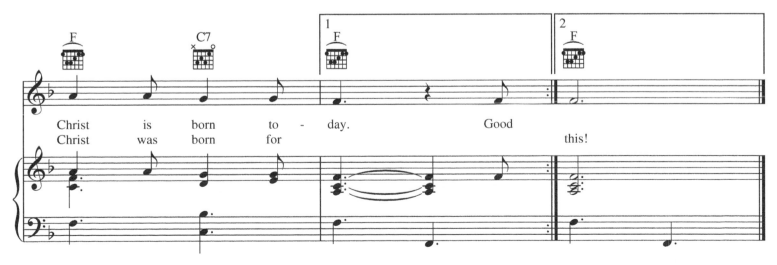

Christ is born to - day. Good
Christ was born for this!

GOOD KING WENCESLAS

Words by JOHN M. NEALE
Music from *Piae Cantiones*

With spirit

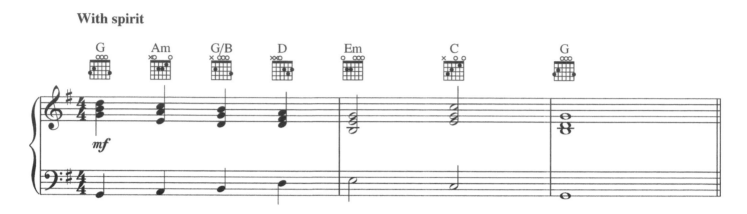

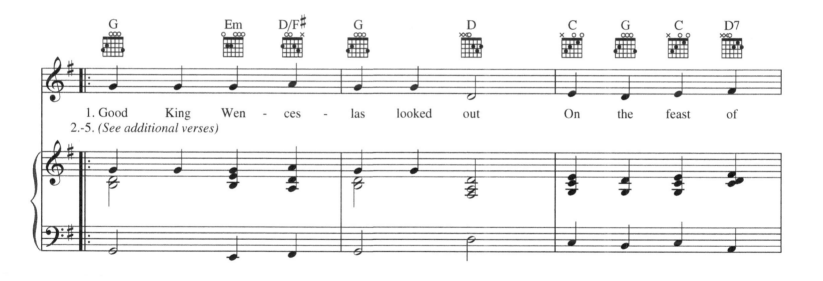

1. Good King Wen - ces - las looked out On the feast of
2.-5. *(See additional verses)*

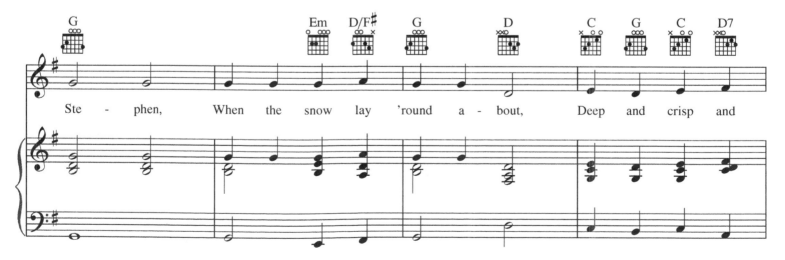

Ste - phen, When the snow lay 'round a - bout, Deep and crisp and

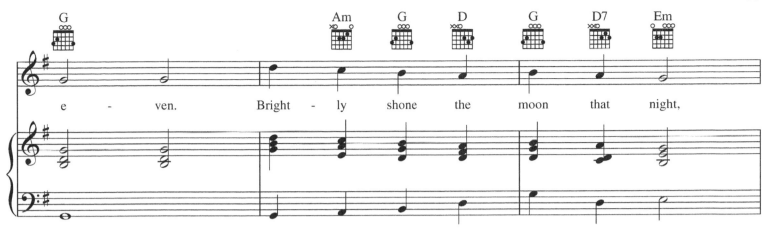

e - ven. Bright - ly shone the moon that night,

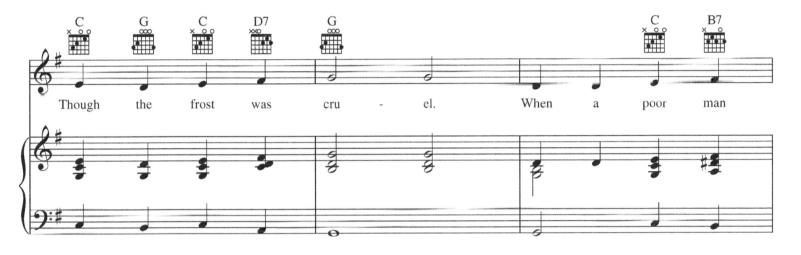

Though the frost was cru - el. When a poor man

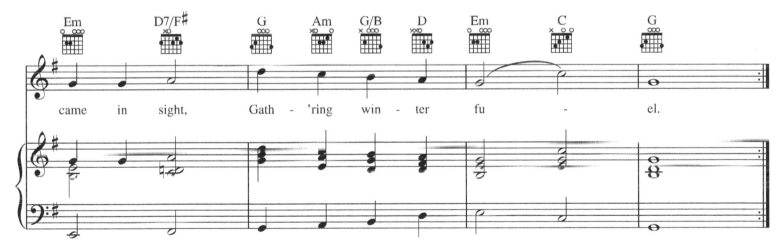

came in sight, Gath - 'ring win - ter fu - el.

Additional Verses

2. "Hither page, and stand by me,
   If thou know'st it, telling,
   Yonder peasant, who is he?
   Where and what his dwelling?"
   "Sire, he lives a good league hence,
   Underneath the mountain;
   Right against the forest fence,
   By Saint Agnes' fountain."

3. "Bring me flesh, and bring me wine,
   Bring me pine-logs hither;
   Thou and I will see him dine,
   When we bear them thither."
   Page and monarch forth they went,
   Forth they went together;
   Through the rude winds wild lament:
   And the bitter weather.

4. "Sire, the night is darker now,
   And the wind blows stronger;
   Fails my heart, I know not how,
   I can go no longer."
   "Mark my footsteps, my good page,
   Tred thou in them boldly:
   Thou shalt find the winter's rage
   Freeze thy blood less coldly."

5. In his master's steps he trod,
   Where the snow lay dinted;
   Heat was in the very sod
   Which the saint had printed.
   Therefore, Christian men, be sure,
   Wealth or rank possessing,
   Ye who now will bless the poor,
   Shall yourselves find blessing.

THE HAPPY CHRISTMAS COMES ONCE MORE

Words by NICOLAI F.S. GRUNDTVIG
Music by C. BALLE

Flowing Waltz (not too fast)

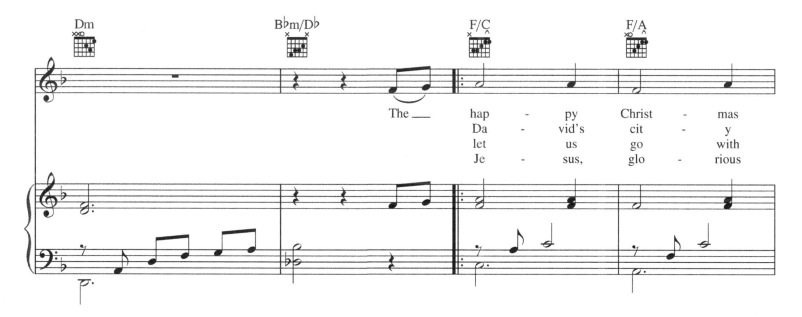

The ___ hap - py Christ - mas
Da - vid's cit - y
Je - sus, glo - rious

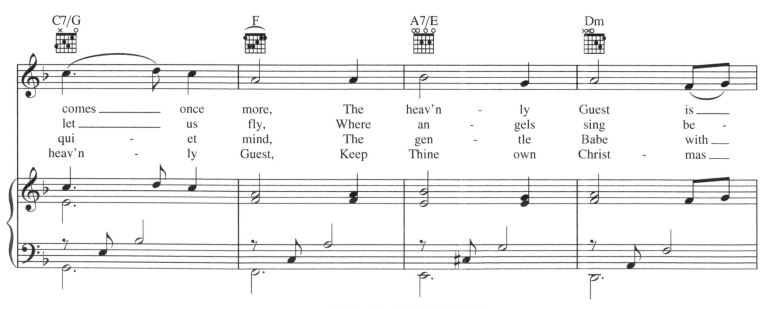

comes ___ once more, The heav'n - ly Guest is ___
let ___ us fly, Where an - gels sing be -
qui - et mind, The an - gen - tle Babe with ___
heav'n - ly Guest, Keep Thine own Christ - mas ___

at _____ the door, The bless - ed
neath _____ the sky, Through plain _____ and
shep - herds find, To gaze _____ on
in _____ our breast; Then Da - vid's

words the shep - herds thrill, The joy - ous
vil - lage press - ing near, And news from
Him who glad - dens them, The lov - liest
harp - string, hushed ____ so long, Shall swell our

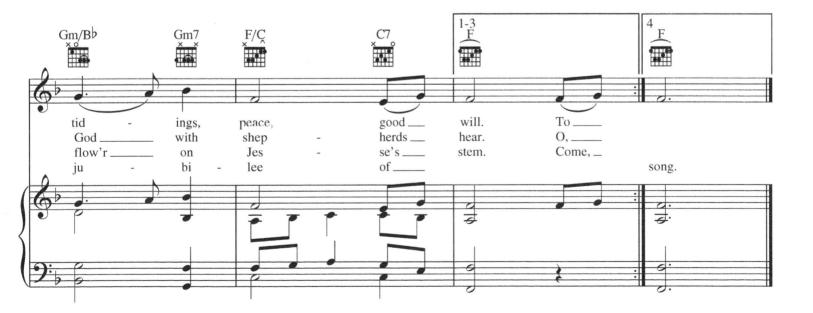

tid - ings, peace, good ___ will. To ___
God _____ with shep - herds ___ hear. O, ___
flow'r ___ on Jes - se's ___ stem. Come, ___
ju - bi - lee of ___ song.

HARK! THE HERALD ANGELS SING

Words by CHARLES WESLEY
Altered by GEORGE WHITEFIELD
Music by FELIX MENDELSSOHN-BARTHOLDY

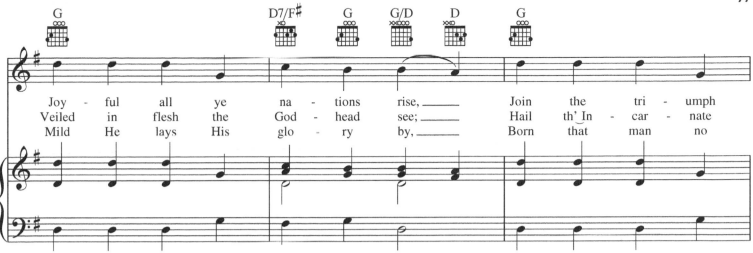

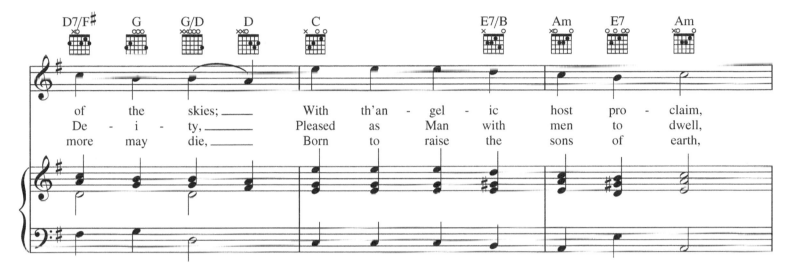

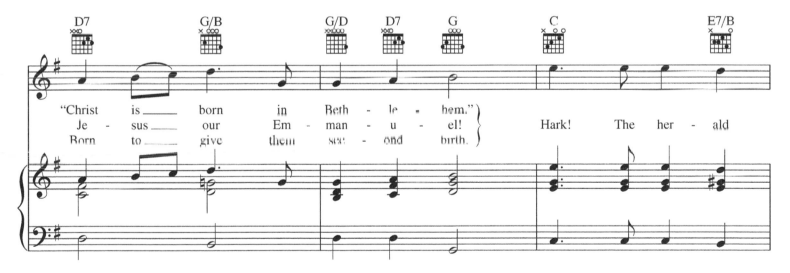

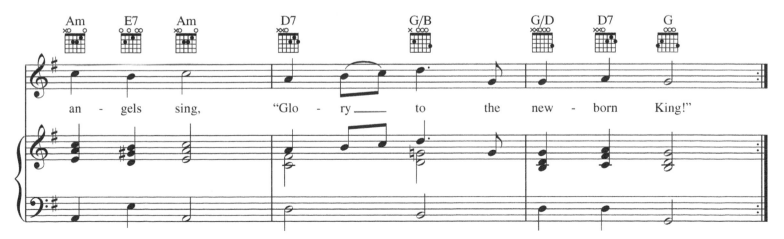

HE IS BORN, THE HOLY CHILD

Traditional French Carol

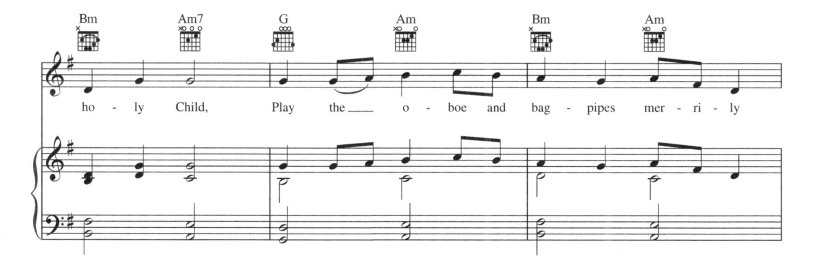

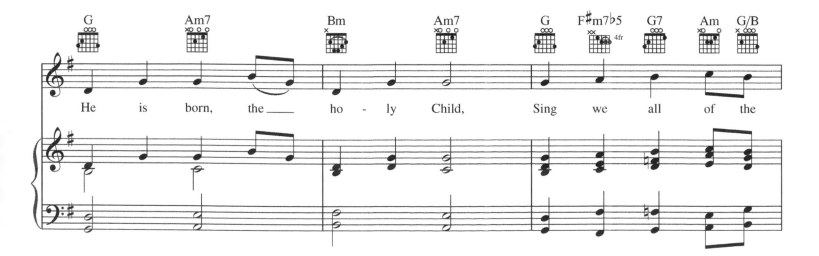

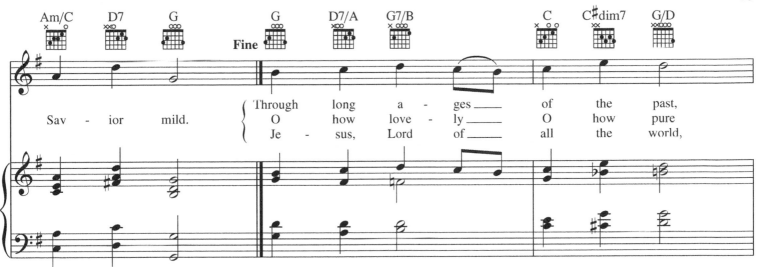

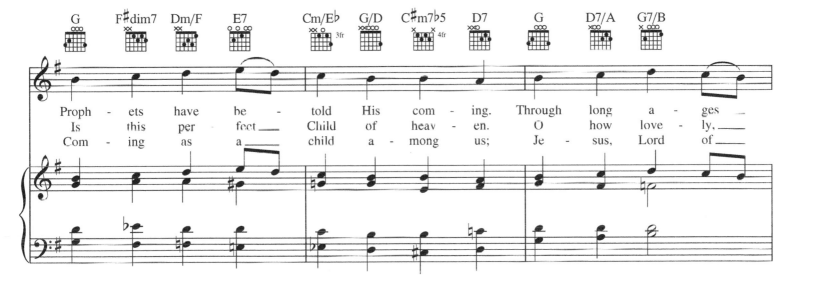

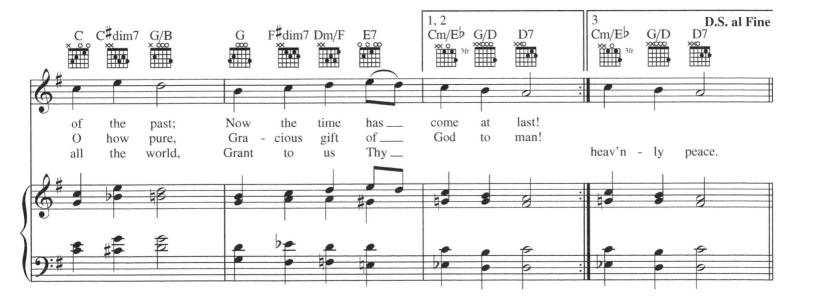

HERE WE COME A-WASSAILING

Traditional

Brightly

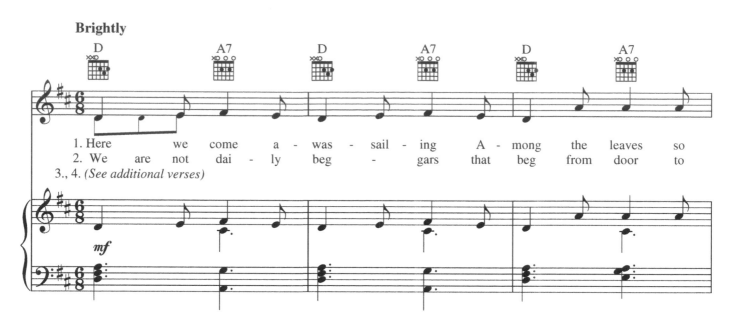

1. Here we come a-was-sail-ing A-mong the leaves so
2. We are not dai-ly beg-gars that beg from door to
3., 4. *(See additional verses)*

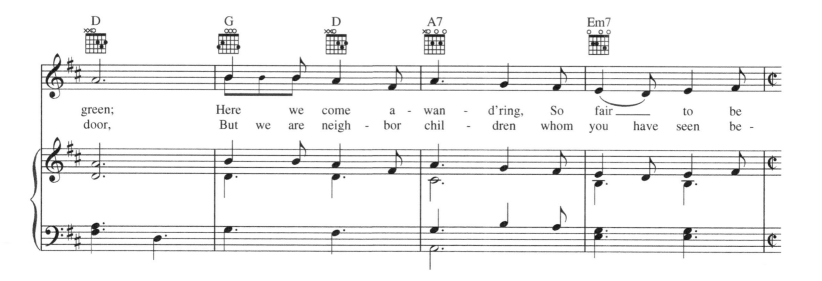

green; Here we come a-wan-d'ring, So fair to be
door, But we are neigh-bor chil-dren whom you have seen be-

$(\ \cdot = \ \ )$ **Refrain**

seen.} Love and joy come to you, And to you your was-sail
fore:}

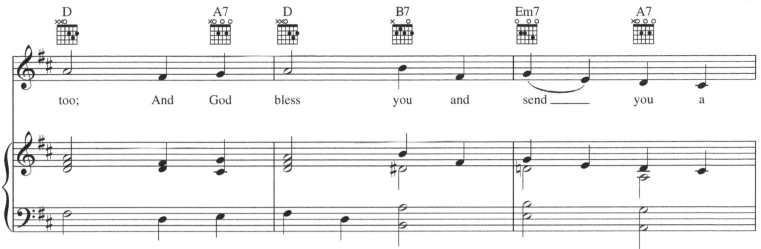

too; And God bless you and send _____ you a

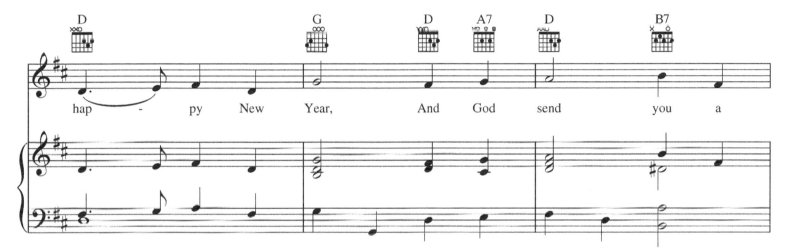

hap - py New Year, And God send you a

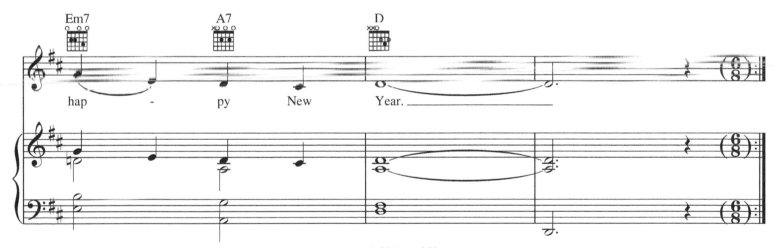

hap - py New Year. _____

Additional Verses

3. We have got a little purse
   Of stretching leather skin;
   We want a little money
   To line it well within:
   Refrain

4. God bless the master of this house,
   Likewise the mistress too;
   And all the little children
   That round the table go:
   Refrain

THE HOLLY AND THE IVY

18th Century English Carol

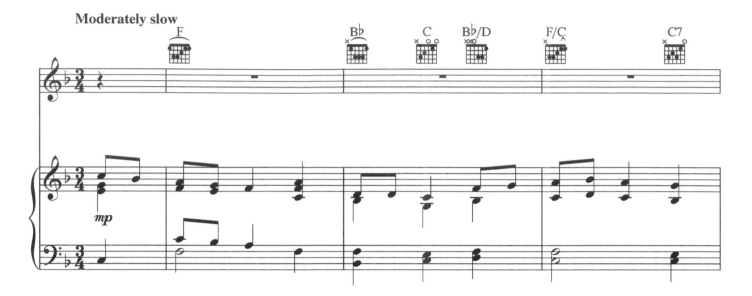

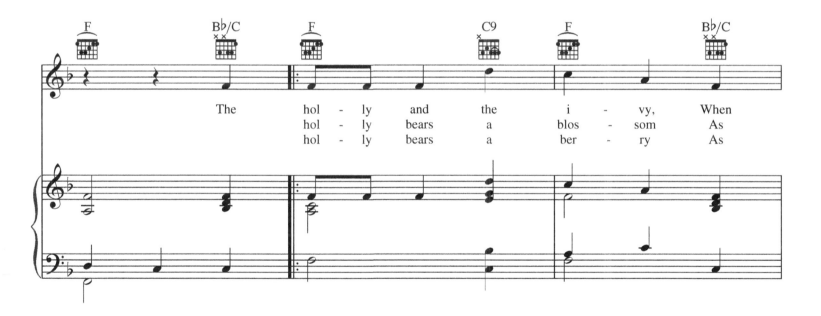

The hol - ly and the i - vy, When
hol - ly bears a blos - som As
hol - ly bears a ber - ry As

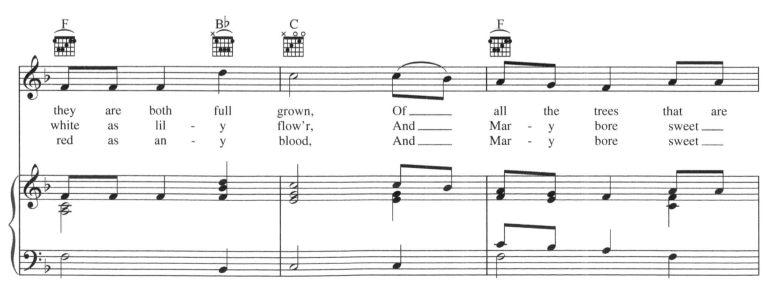

they are both full grown, Of _____ all the trees that are
white as lil - y flow'r, And _____ Mar - y bore sweet _____
red as an - y blood, And _____ Mar - y bore sweet _____

I AM SO GLAD ON CHRISTMAS EVE

Words by MARIE WEXELSEN
Music by PEDER KNUDSEN

am so glad _____ on Christ - mas Eve, The night of Je - sus'
am so glad _____ on Christ - mas Eve, My prais - es rise _____ a -

birth; _____ That's when a star _____ shone like the sun, And
bove _____ To Je - sus who _____ has brought to earth And The

an - gels sang _____ on earth. _____ I
Par - a - dise _____ of Love. _____

I HEARD THE BELLS ON CHRISTMAS DAY

Words by HENRY WADSWORTH LONGFELLOW
Music by JOHN BAPTISTE CALKIN

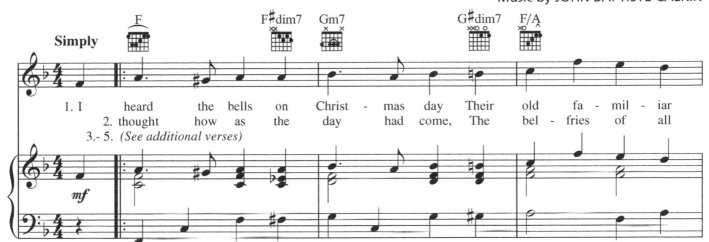

1. I heard the bells on Christ - mas day Their old fa - mil - iar
2. thought how as the day had come, The bel - fries of all
3.- 5. *(See additional verses)*

car - ols play; And mild and sweet the words re - peat, Of
Christ - en - dom Had rolled a - long th' un - bro - ken song Of

peace on earth, good will to men. I will to men!
peace on earth, good will to men. And

Additional Verses

3. And in despair I bowed my head:
   "There is no peace on earth," I said,
   "For hate is strong, and mocks the song
   Of peace on earth, good will to men."

4. Then pealed the bells more loud and deep:
   "God is not dead, nor doth He sleep;
   The wrong shall fail, the right prevail,
   With peace on earth, good will to men."

5. Till, ringing, singing on its way,
   The world revolved from night to day,
   A voice, a chime, a chant sublime,
   Of peace on earth, good will to men!

I SAW THREE SHIPS

Traditional English Carol

IN THE FIELD WITH THEIR FLOCKS ABIDING

Traditional

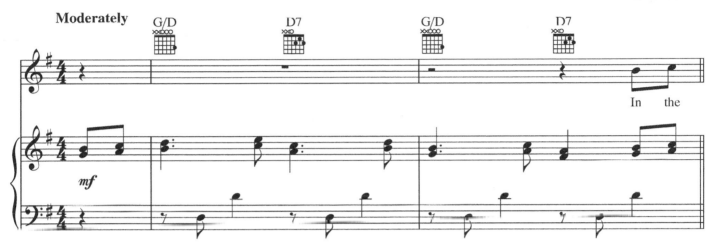

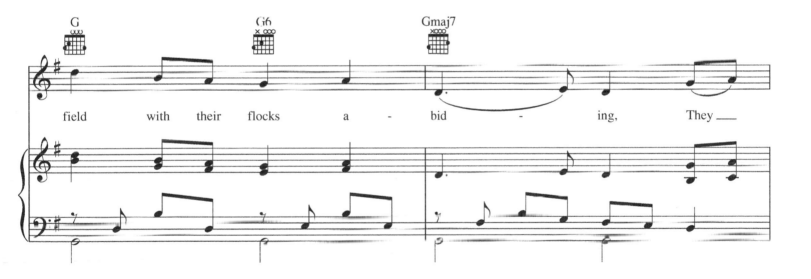

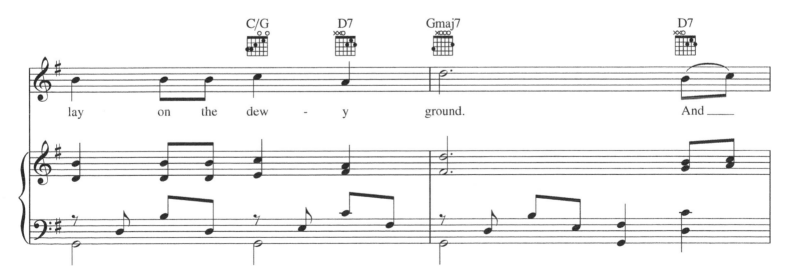

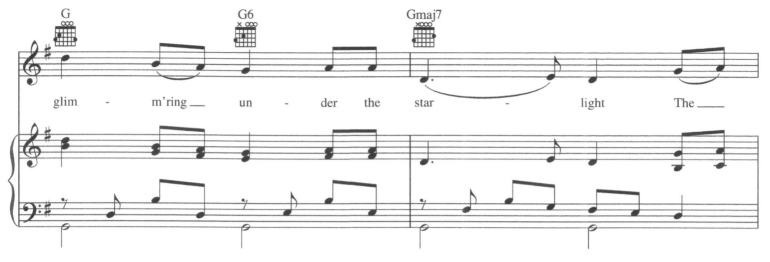

glim - m'ring _ un - der the star - light The _

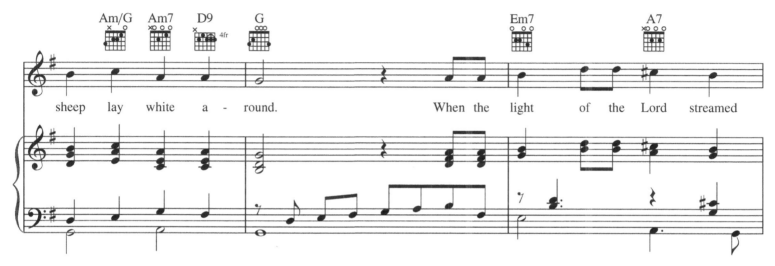

sheep lay white a - round. When the light of the Lord streamed

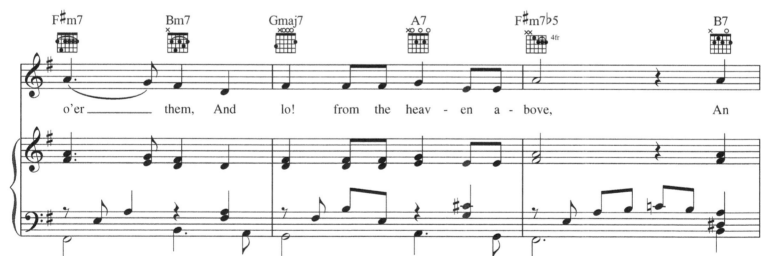

o'er _ them, And lo! from the heav - en a - bove, An

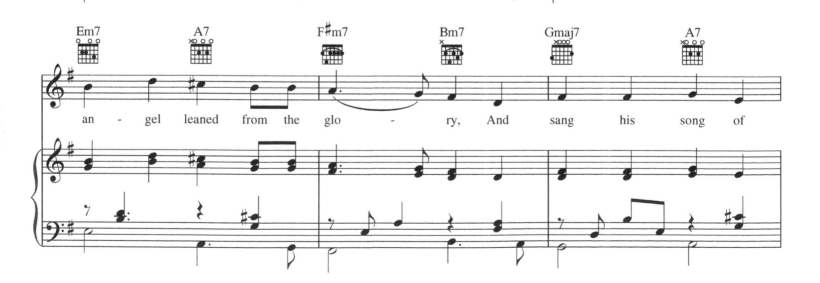

an - gel leaned from the glo - ry, And sang his song of

love. He sang that first sweet Christ - mas, The

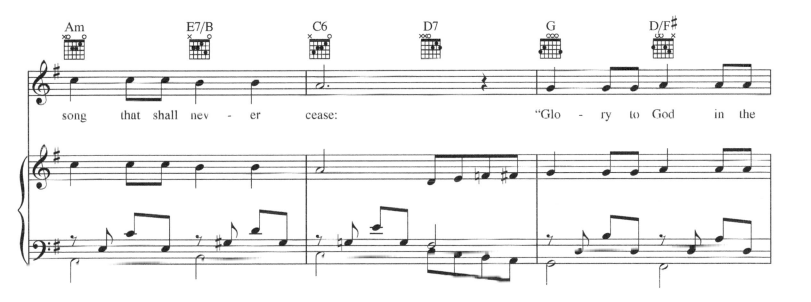

song that shall nev - er cease: "Glo - ry to God in the

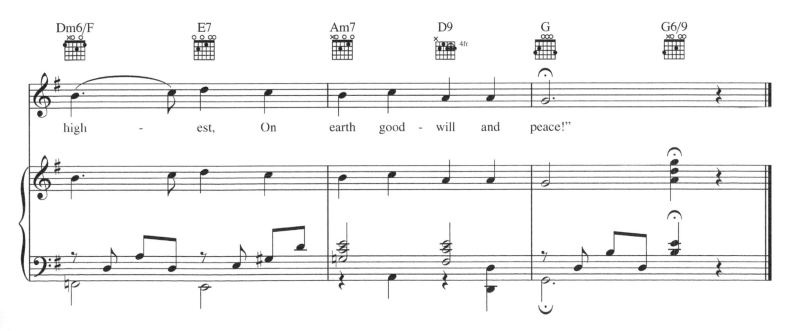

high - est, On earth good - will and peace!"

IN THE SILENCE OF THE NIGHT

Traditional Carol

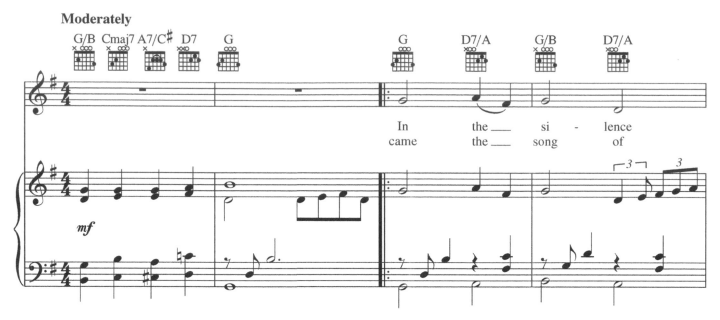

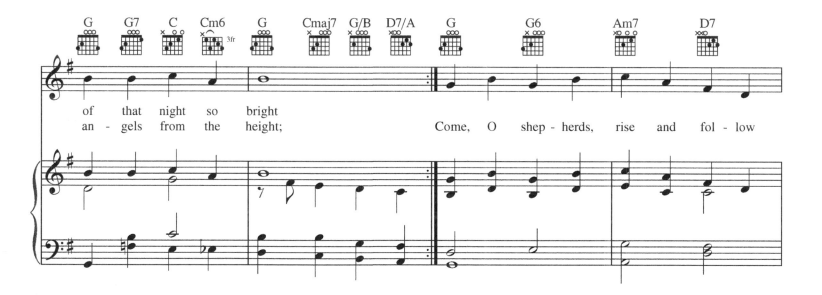

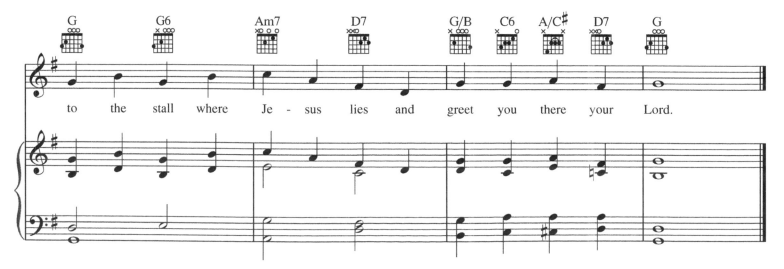

IT CAME UPON THE MIDNIGHT CLEAR

Words by EDMUND HAMILTON SEARS
Music by RICHARD STORRS WILLIS

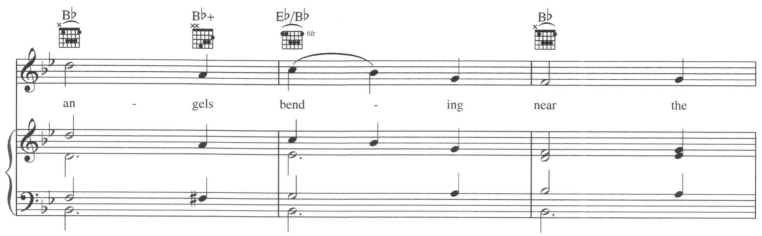

an - gels bend - ing near the

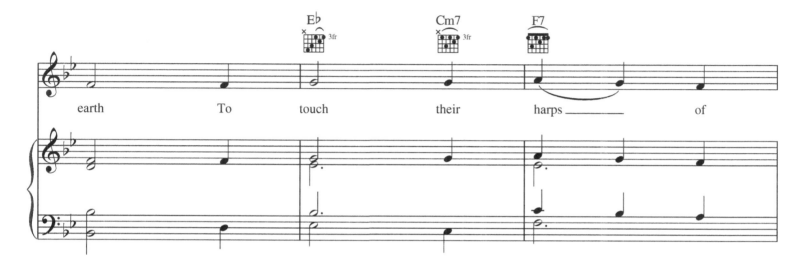

earth To touch their harps _____ of

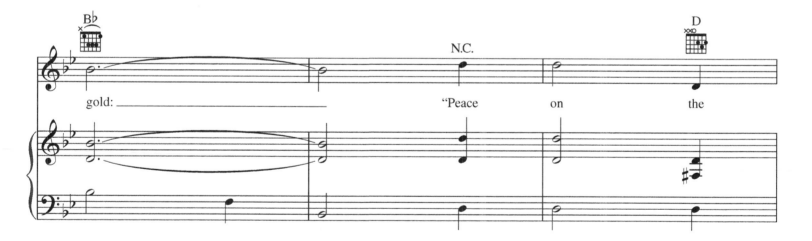

gold: _____ "Peace on the

earth, _____ good will to men, From

heav'n's _____ all - gra - cious King." _____

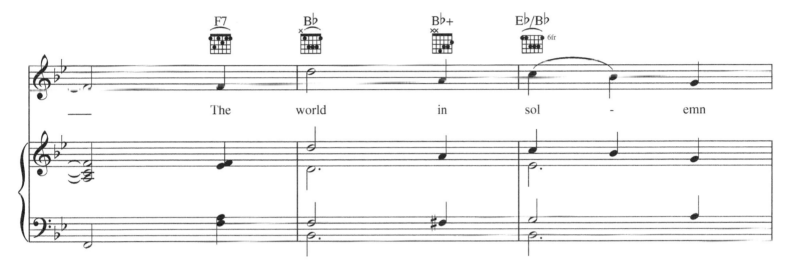

_____ The world in sol - emn

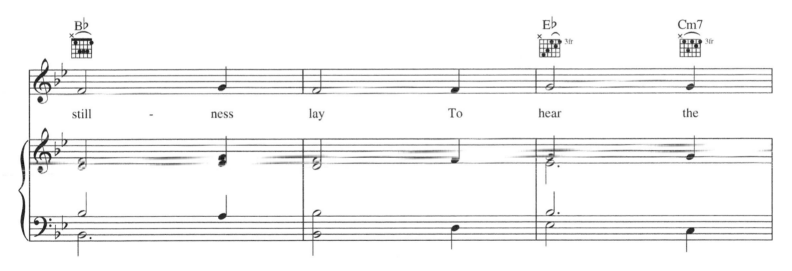

still - ness lay To hear the

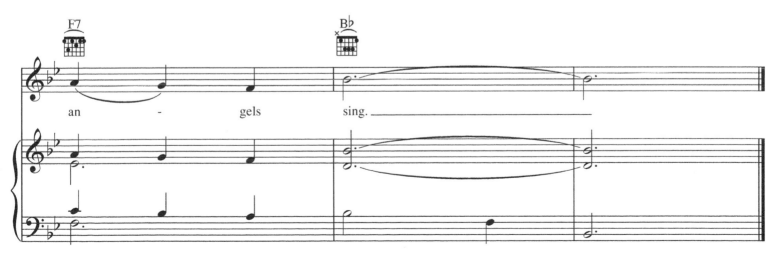

an - gels sing. _____

JESU, JOY OF MAN'S DESIRING

By JOHANN SEBASTIAN BACH

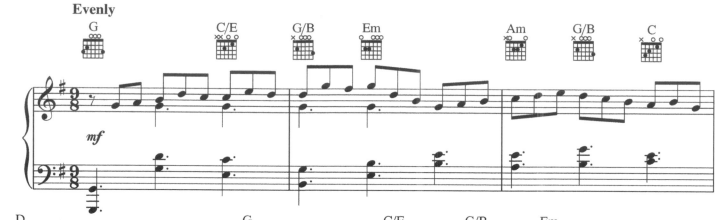

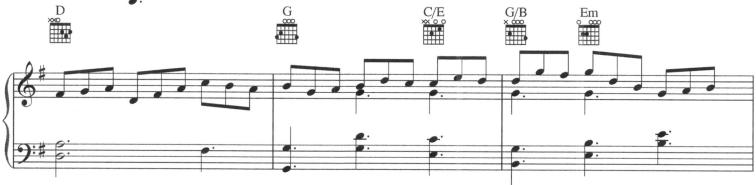

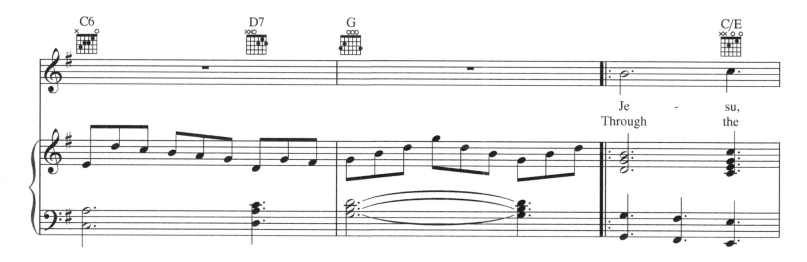

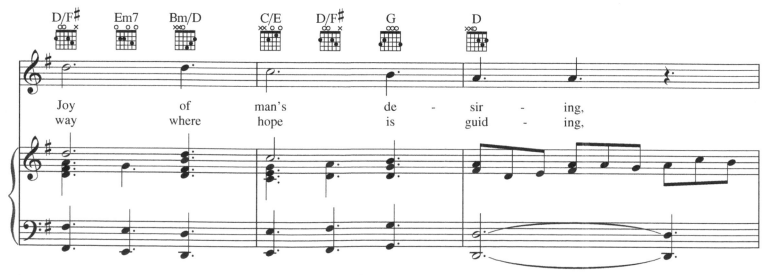

Ho - ly wis - dom,
Hark, what peace - ful

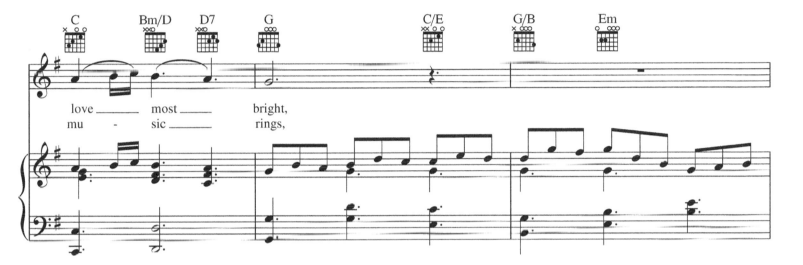

love _____ most _____ bright,
mu - sic _____ rings,

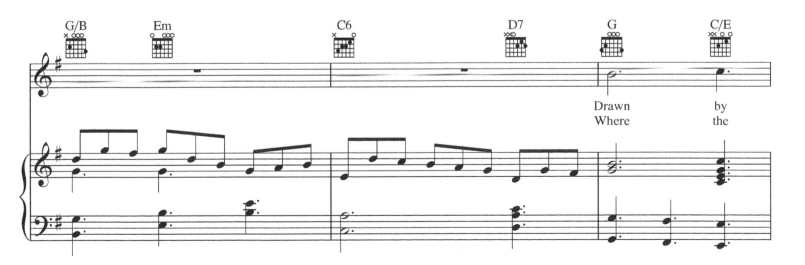

Drawn by
Where the

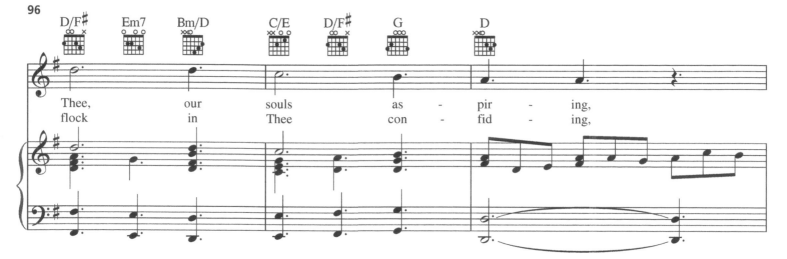

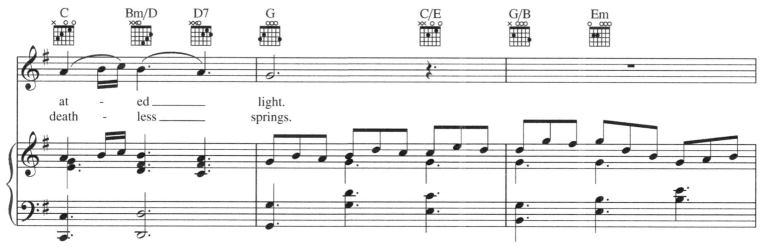

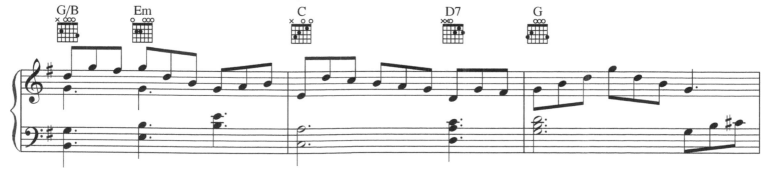

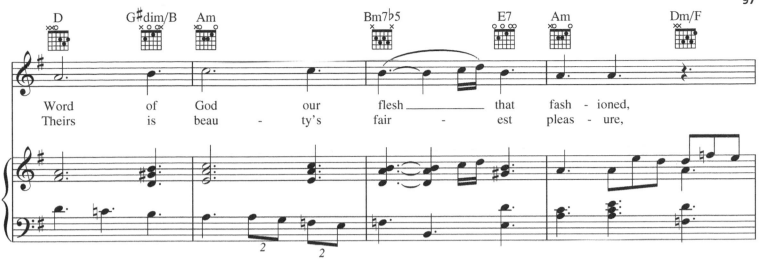

Word of God our flesh _____ that fash - ioned,
Theirs is beau - ty's fair - est pleas - ure,

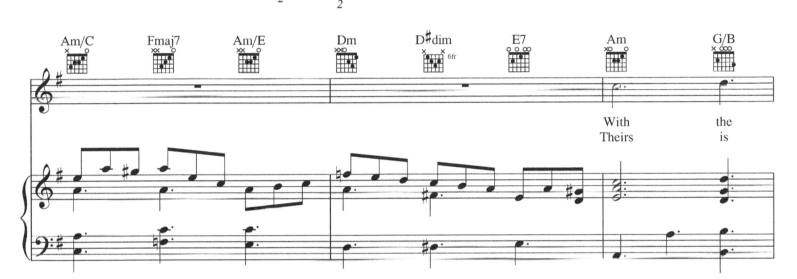

With the
Theirs is

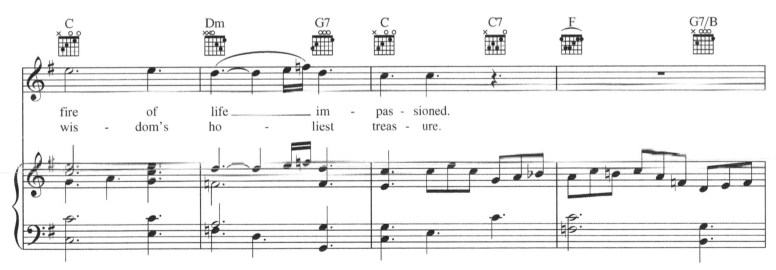

fire of life _____ im - pas - sioned.
wis - dom's ho - liest treas - ure.

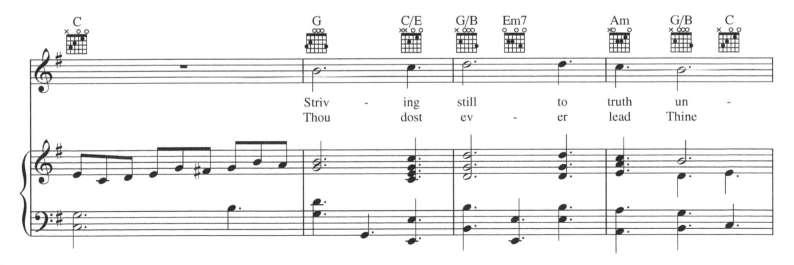

Striv - ing still to truth un -
Thou dost ev - er lead Thine

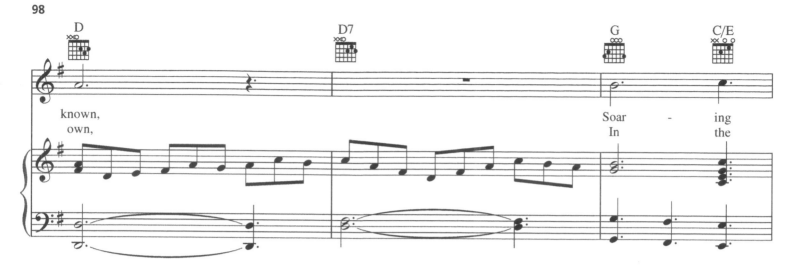

known,
own,

Soar - ing
In - the

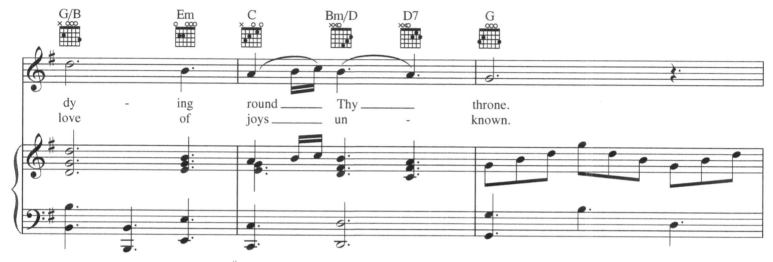

dy - ing round _____ Thy _____ throne.
love of joys _____ un - known.

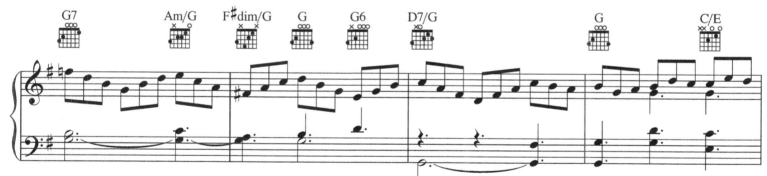

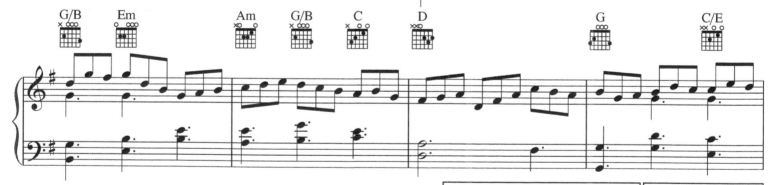

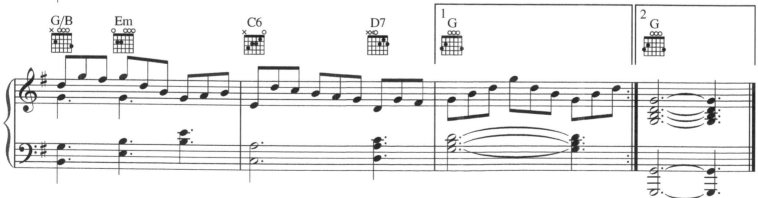

MASTERS IN THIS HALL

Traditional English

Now - ell, Now - ell, Now - ell! Now - ell sing we
Now - ell, Now - ell, Now - ell! Now - ell sing we

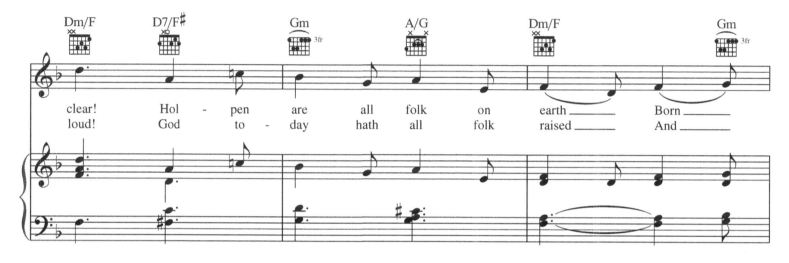

clear! Hol - pen are all folk on earth_____ Born_____
loud! God to - day hath all on folk raised_____ And_____

is God's Son, so dear. cast a - down the proud.

This is Christ, the Lord;_____ Mas - ters, be ye glad!_____

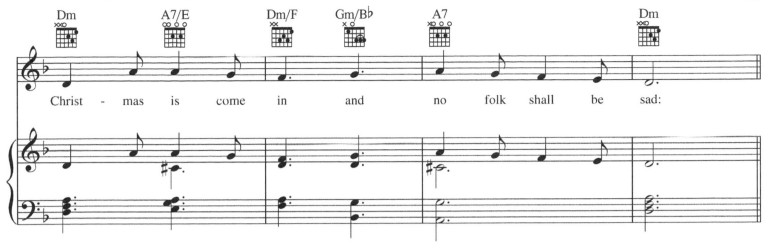

Christ - mas is come in and no folk shall be sad:

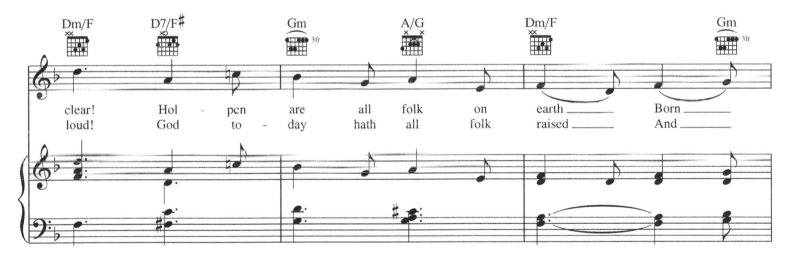

Now - ell, Now - ell, Now - ell! Now - ell sing we
Now - ell, Now - ell, Now - ell! Now - ell sing we

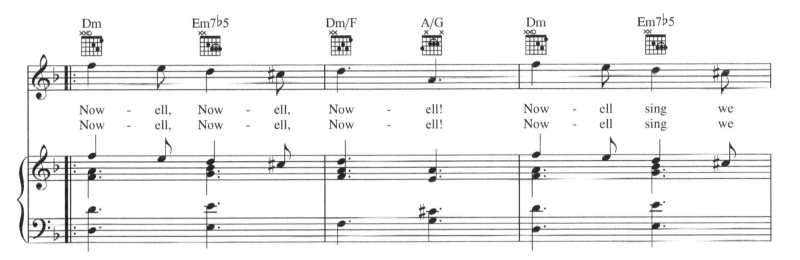

clear! Hol - pen are all folk on earth_____ Born_____
loud! God to - day hath all on folk raised_____ And_____

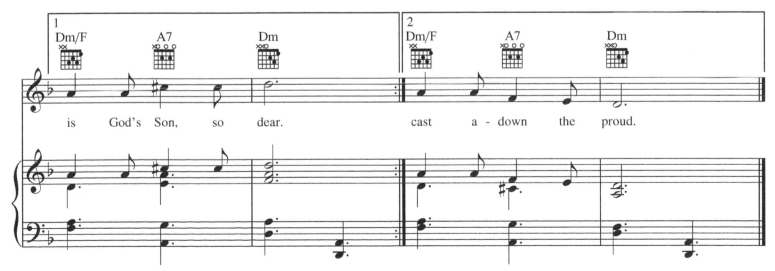

is God's Son, so dear.   cast a - down the proud.

JESUS HOLY, BORN SO LOWLY

Traditional Polish

Like a lullaby

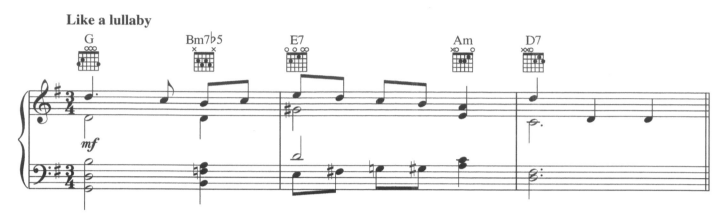

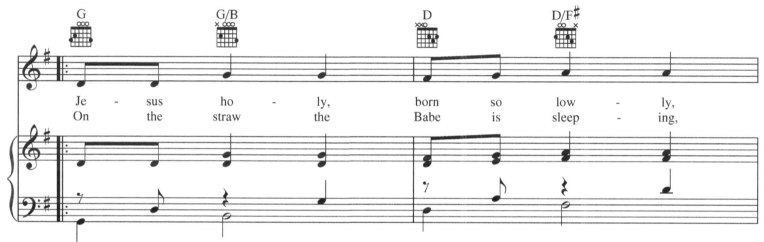

Je - sus ho - ly, born so low - ly,
On the straw the Babe is sleep - ing,

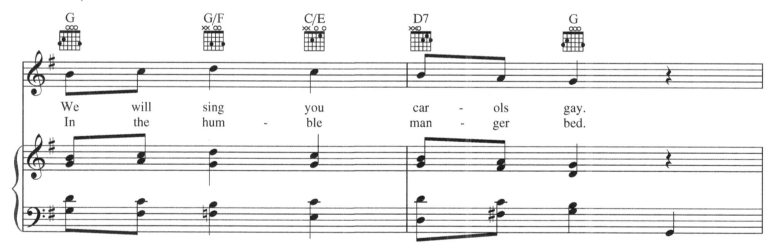

We will sing you car - ols gay.
In the hum - ble man - ger bed.

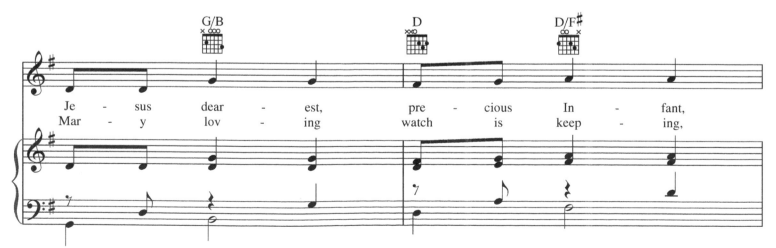

Je - sus dear - est, pre - cious In - fant,
Mar - y lov - ing watch is keep - ing,

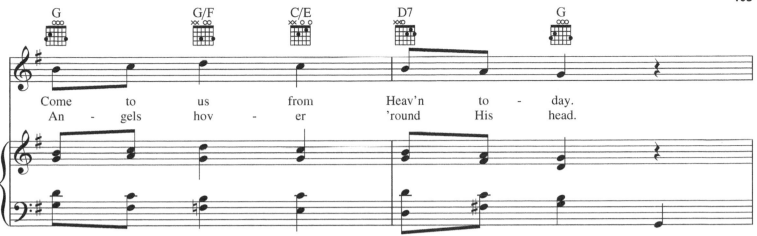

Come to us from Heav'n to-day.
An - gels hov - er 'round His head.

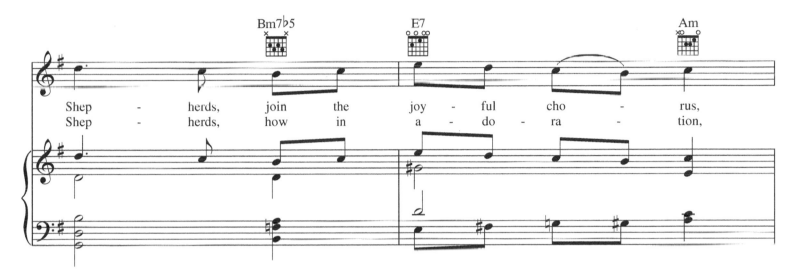

Shep - herds, join the joy - ful cho - rus,
Shep - herds, how in a - do - ra - tion,

Heav'n - ly love is reign - ing o'er____ us,
Prais - ing God's sweet be - ne - dic - tion,

Here ap - pear - ing as a Babe.
That up - on the earth is shed.

JOY TO THE WORLD

Words by ISAAC WATTS
Music by GEORGE FRIDERIC HANDEL
Arranged by LOWELL MASON

With spirit

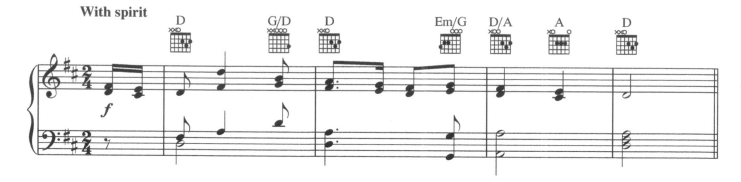

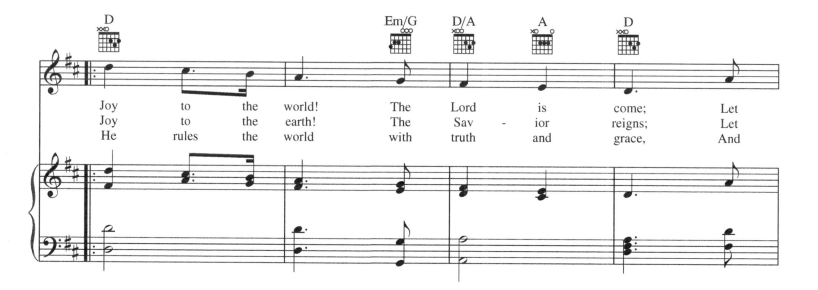

Joy to the world! The Lord is come; Let
Joy to the earth! The Sav - ior reigns; Let
He rules the world with truth and grace, And

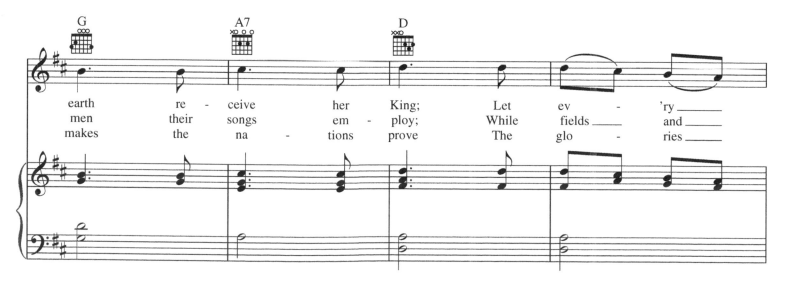

earth re - ceive her King; Let ev - 'ry _____
men their songs em - ploy; While fields _____ and _____
makes the na - tions prove The glo - ries _____

heart _____ pre - pare _____ Him _____ room, _____ and heav'n and na - ture _____
floods, _____ rocks, hills _____ and _____ plains _____ Re - peat the sound - ing _____
of _____ His right - eous - ness _____ And won - ders of His _____

A

sing, _____ And _____ heav'n and na - ture _____ sing, _____ And _____
joy, _____ Re - peat the sound - ing _____ joy, _____ Re -
love, _____ And _____ won - ders of His _____ love, _____ And _____

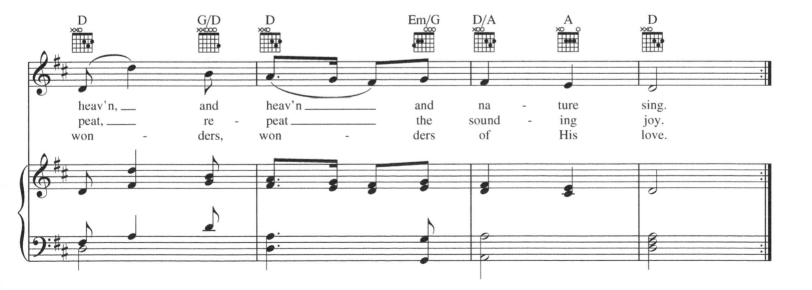

D   G/D   D   Em/G   D/A   A   D

heav'n, _____ and _____ heav'n _____ and na - ture sing.
peat, _____ re - peat _____ the sound - ing _____ joy.
won - ders, won - ders of His _____ love.

LO, HOW A ROSE E'ER BLOOMING

15th Century German Carol
Translated by THEODORE BAKER
Music from *Alte Catholische Geistliche Kirchengesäng*

Lo, how a rose e'er bloom-

ing From ten-der stem____ hath sprung! Of Jes-se's

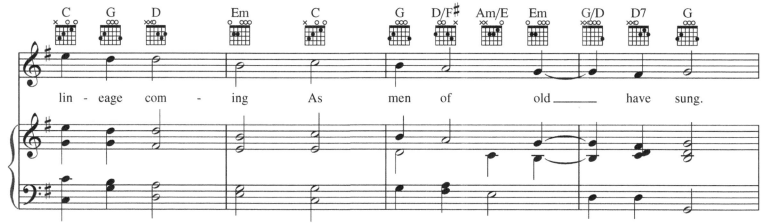

lin-eage com-ing As men of old____ have sung.

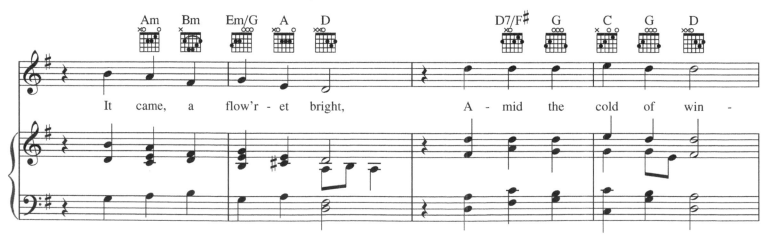

It came, a flow'r-et bright, A-mid the cold of win-

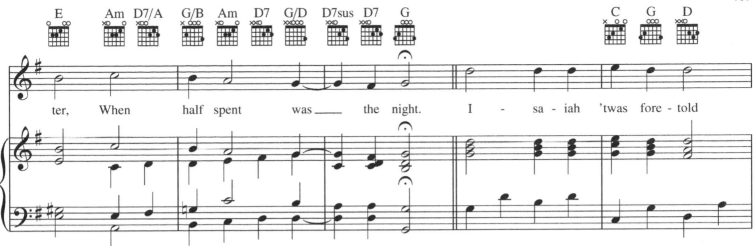

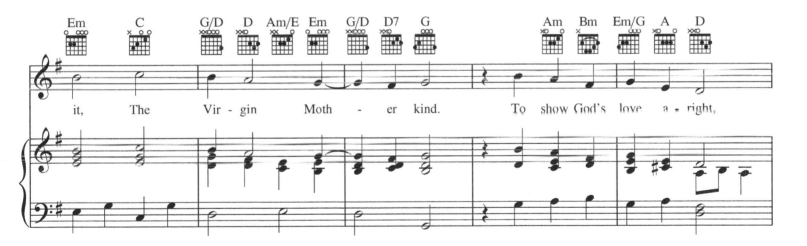

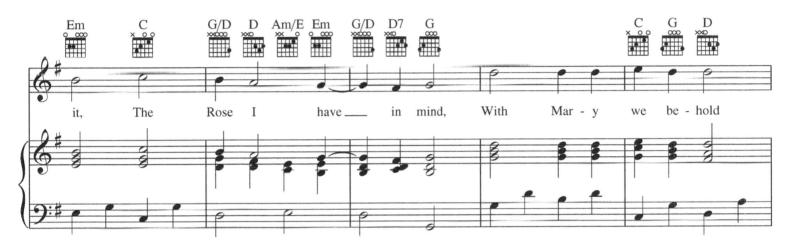

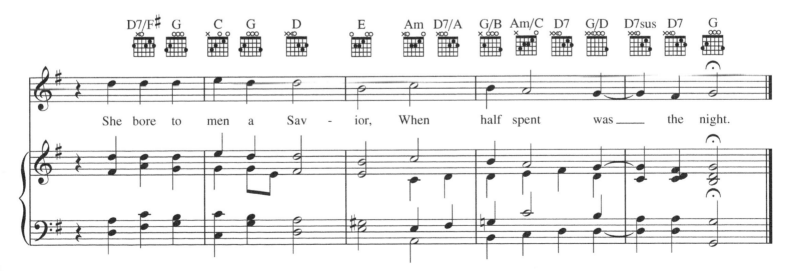

NEIGHBOR, WHAT HAS YOU SO EXCITED?

Traditional French

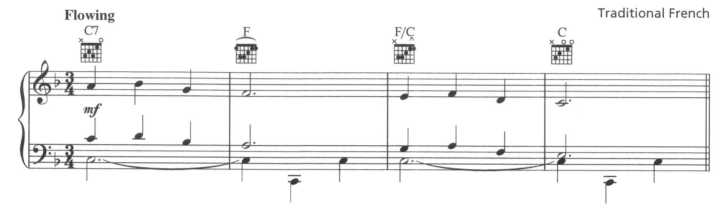

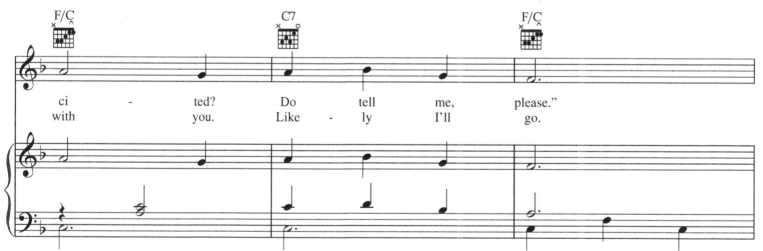

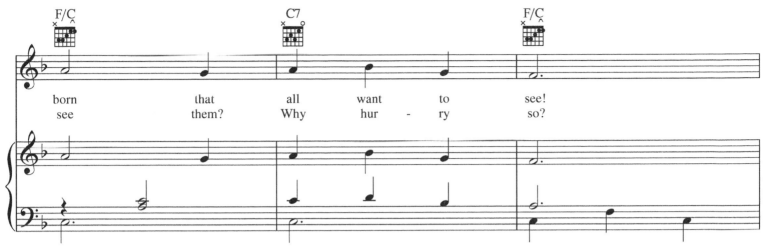

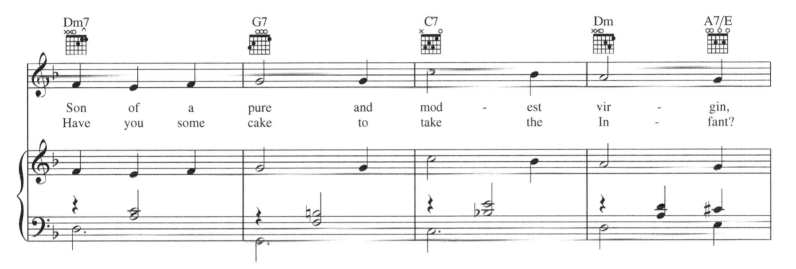

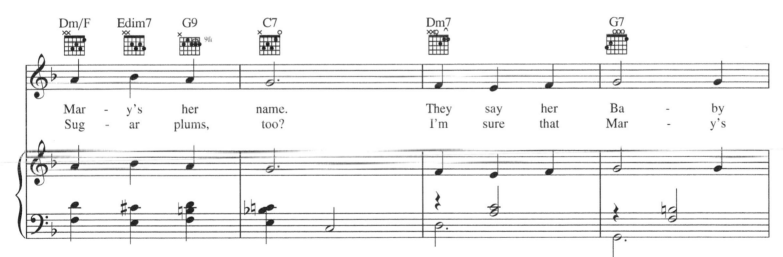

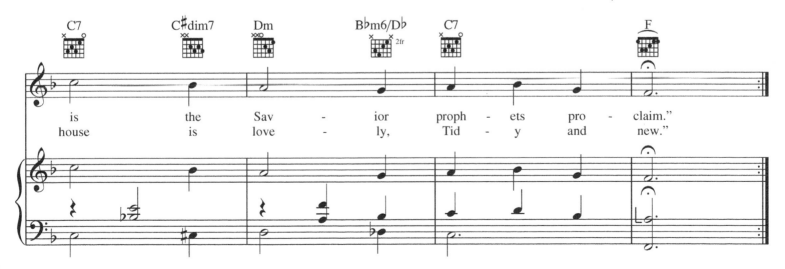

NOËL! NOËL!

French-English Carol

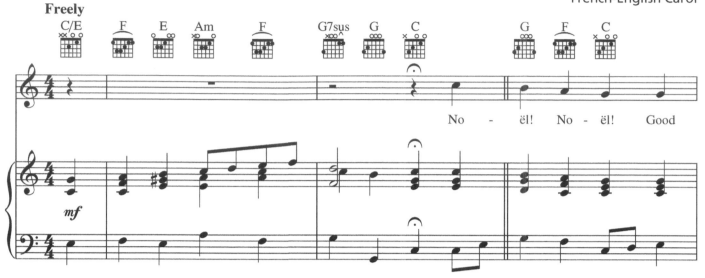

No - ël! No - ël! Good

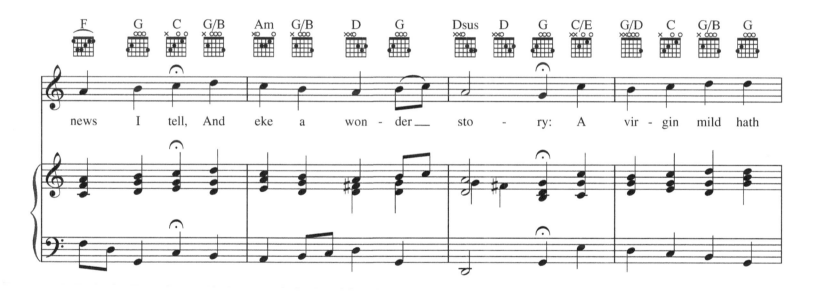

news I tell, And eke a won - der __ sto - ry: A vir - gin mild hath

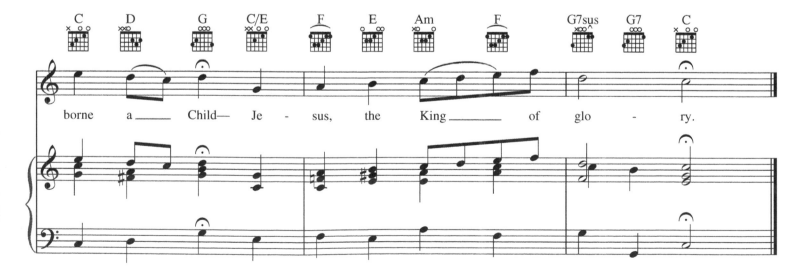

borne a __ Child— Je - sus, the King _____ of glo - ry.

O COME, O COME, IMMANUEL

Plainsong, 13th Century
Words translated by JOHN M. NEALE
and HENRY S. COFFIN

112

ex - ile here Un - til the Son of God _____ ap -

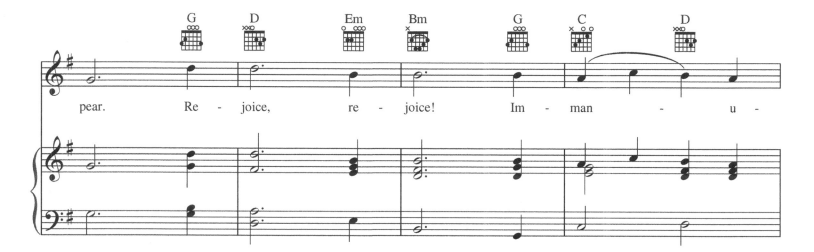

pear. Re - joice, re - joice! Im - man - u -

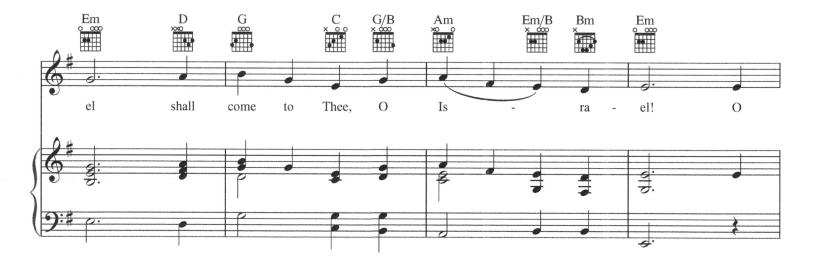

el shall come to Thee, O Is - ra - el! O

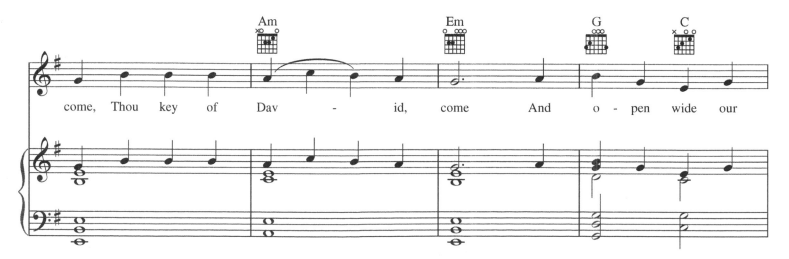

come, Thou key of Dav - id, come And o - pen wide our

113

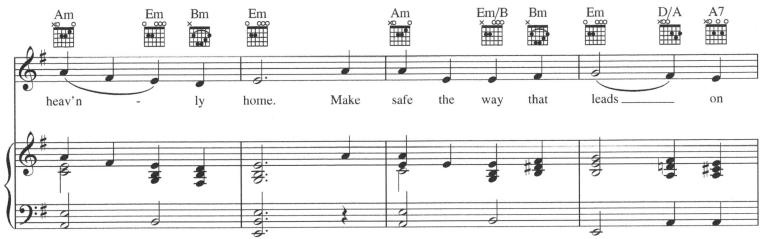

heav'n - ly home. Make safe the way that leads _____ on

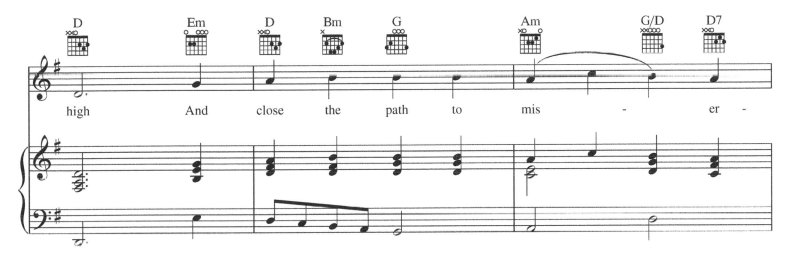

high And close the path to mis - er -

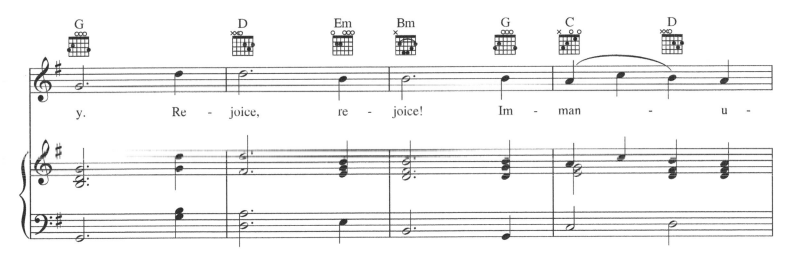

y. Re - joice, re - joice! Im - man - u -

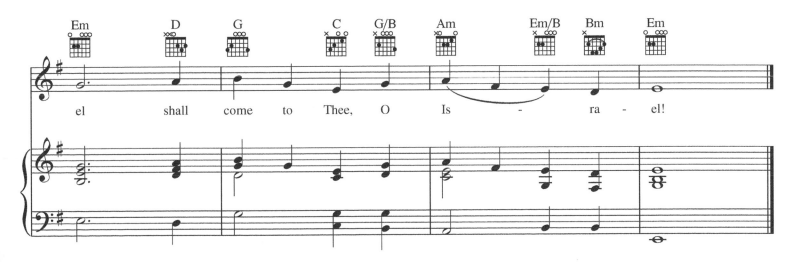

el shall come to Thee, O Is - ra - el!

O BETHLEHEM

Traditional Spanish

Slowly, with expression

mf

O Beth - le - hem,

O'er you a bril - liant star is shin - ing,

O Beth - le - hem. Heav - en - ly choirs of

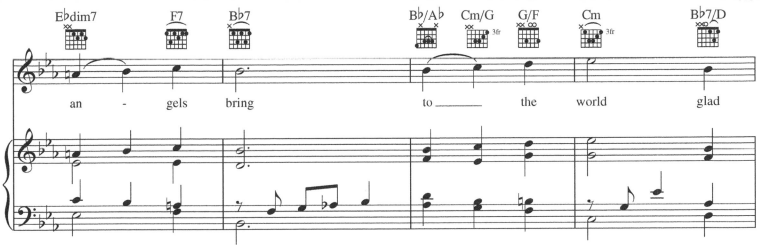

an - gels bring to _____ the world glad

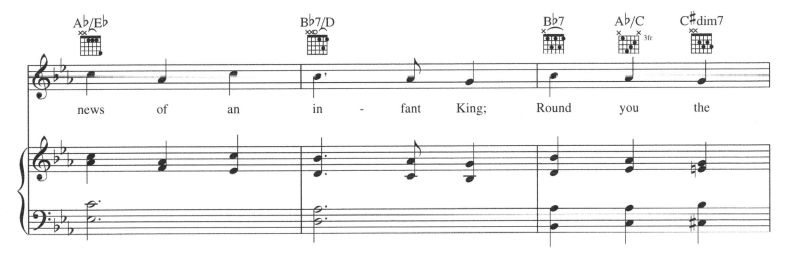

news of an in - fant King; Round you the

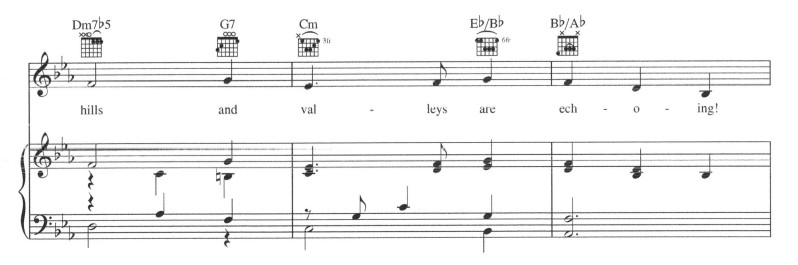

hills and val - leys are ech - o - ing!

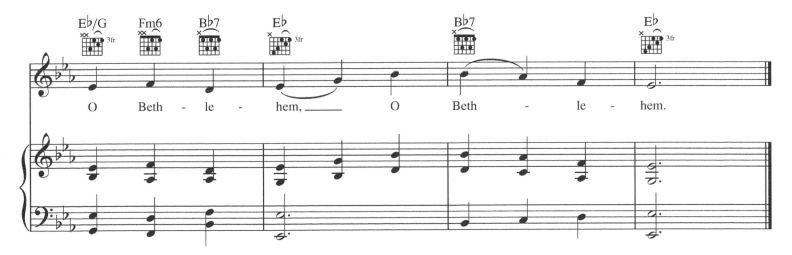

O Beth - le - hem, _____ O Beth - le - hem.

O CHRISTMAS TREE

Traditional German Carol

O Christ - mas tree! O Christ - mas tree, you
Christ - mas tree! O Christ - mas tree, much
Christ - mas tree! O Christ - mas tree, thy

stand in ver - dant beau - ty! O Christ - mas tree, O
pleas - ure doth thou bring me! O Christ - mas tree, O
can - dles shine out bright - ly! O Christ - mas tree, O

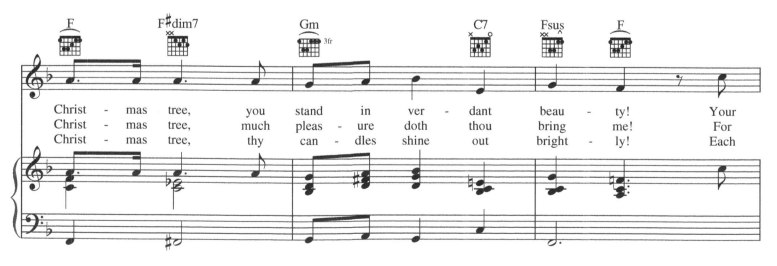

Christ - mas tree, you stand in ver - dant beau - ty! Your
Christ - mas tree, much pleas - ure doth thou bring me! For
Christ - mas tree, thy can - dles shine out bright - ly! Each

O COME, ALL YE FAITHFUL

Words and Music by JOHN FRANCIS WADE
Latin Words translated by FREDERICK OAKELEY

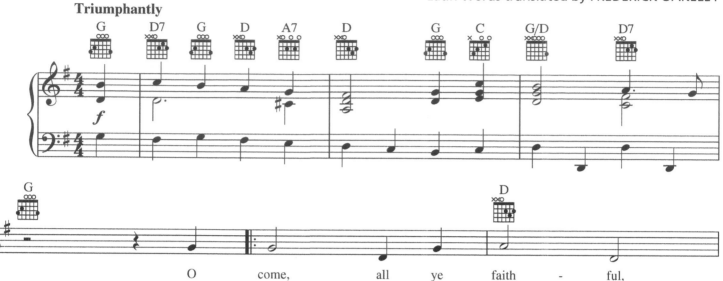

O come, all ye faith - ful,
Sing, all choirs of an - gels,
Yea, Lord, we greet Thee,

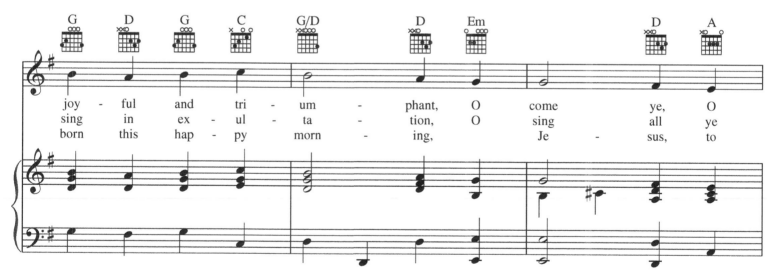

joy - ful and tri - um - phant, O come ye, O
sing in ex - ul - ta - tion, O sing all ye
born this hap - py morn - ing, Je - sus, to

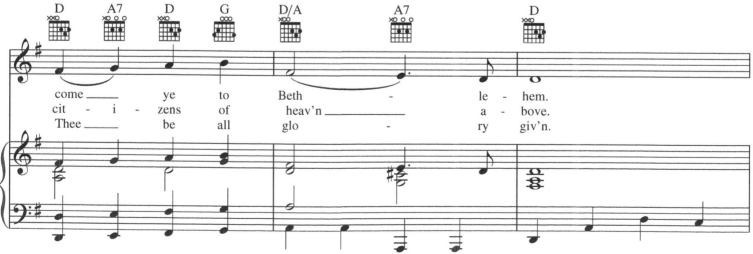

come ____ ye to Beth - le - hem.
cit - i - zens of heav'n ____ a - bove.
Thee ____ be all glo - ry giv'n.

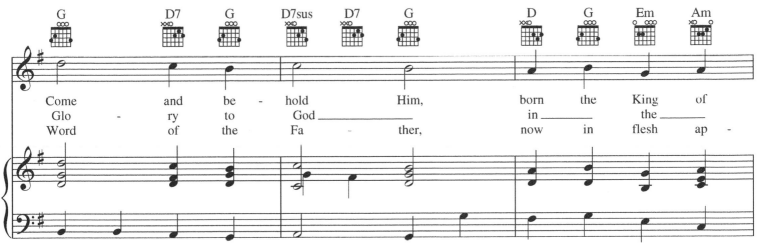

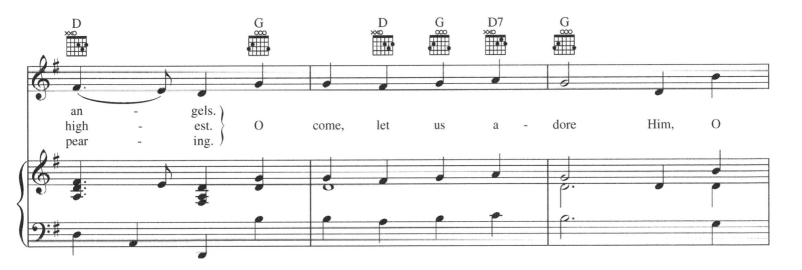

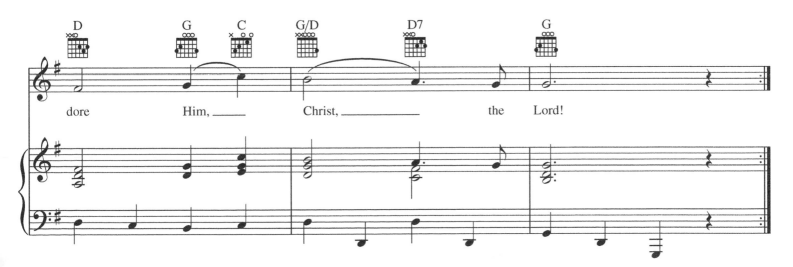

O COME AWAY, YE SHEPHERDS

18th Century French Text
Tune from Air, "Nanon Dormait"

O COME, LITTLE CHILDREN

Words by C. VON SCHMIDT
Music by J.P.A. SCHULZ

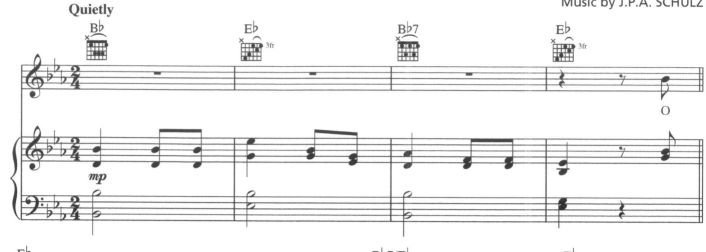

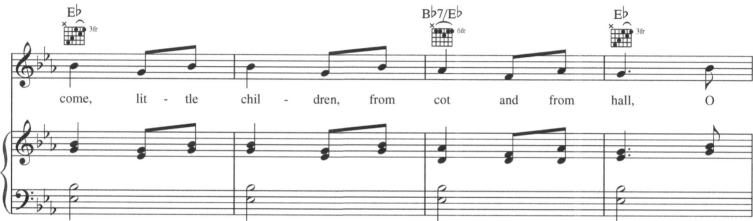

come, lit - tle chil - dren, from cot and from hall, O

come to the man - ger in Beth - le - hem's stall. There

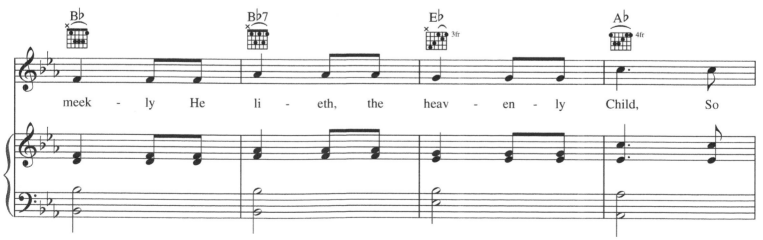

meek - ly He li - eth, the heav - en - ly Child, So

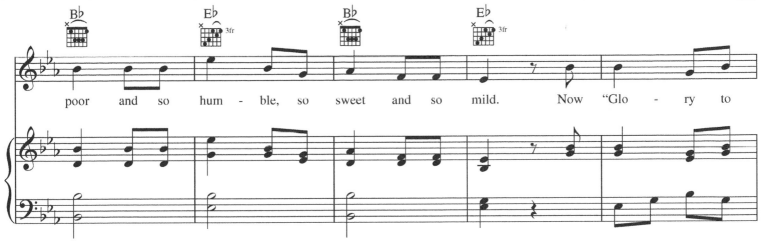

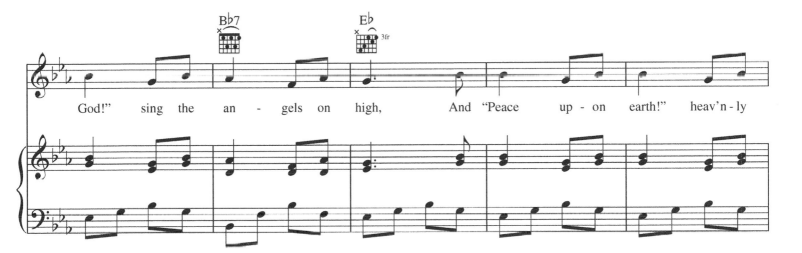

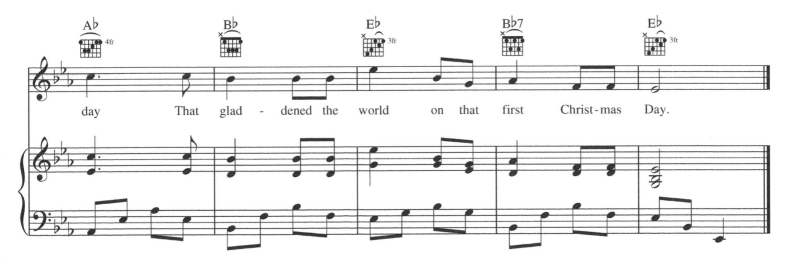

O COME REJOICING

Traditional Polish Carol

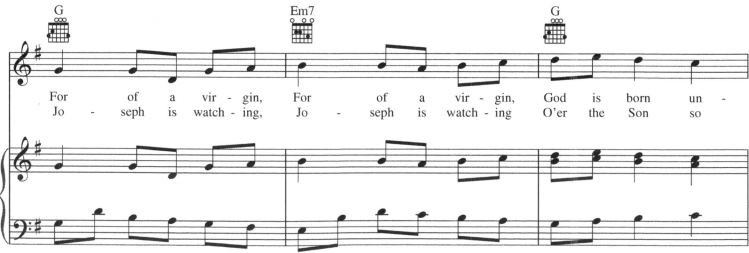

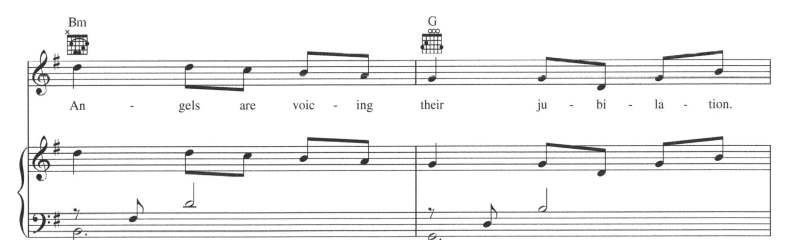

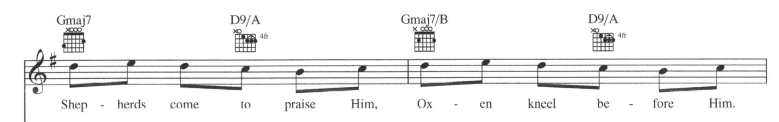

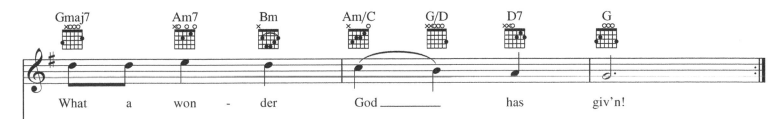

O HOLY NIGHT

French Words by PLACIDE CAPPEAU
English Words by JOHN S. DWIGHT
Music by ADOLPHE ADAM

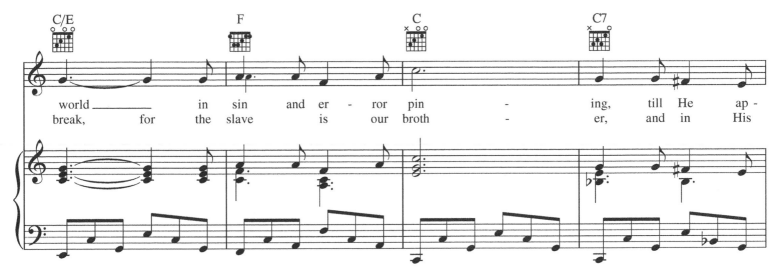

world _____ in sin and er - ror pin - ing, till He ap -
break, for the slave is our broth - er, and in His

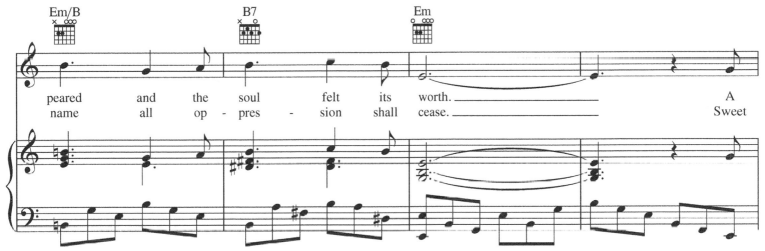

peared and the soul felt its worth. _____ A
name all op - pres - sion shall cease. _____ Sweet

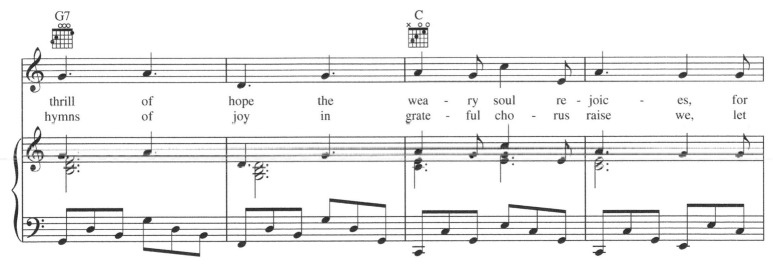

thrill of hope the wea - ry soul re - joic - es, for
hymns of joy in grate - ful cho - rus raise we, let

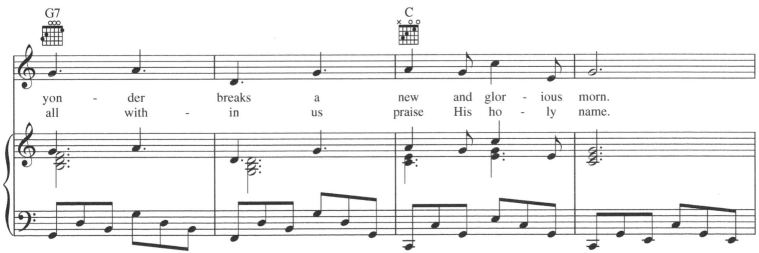

yon - der breaks a new and glor - ious morn.
all with - in us praise His ho - ly name.

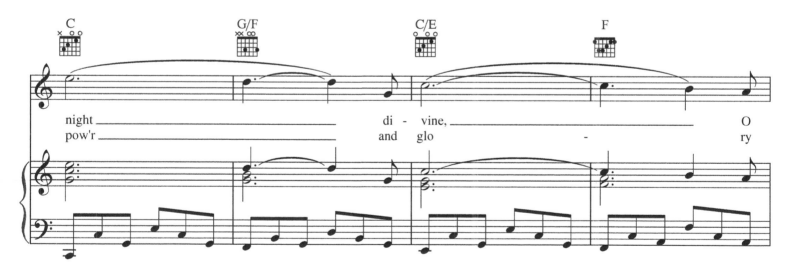

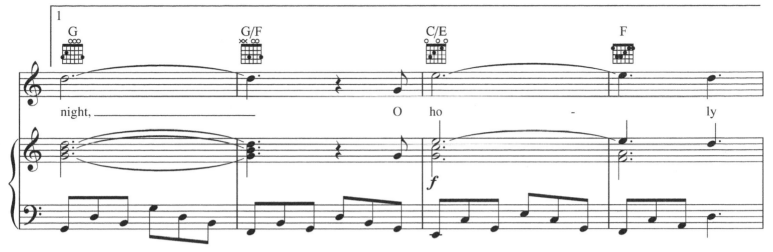

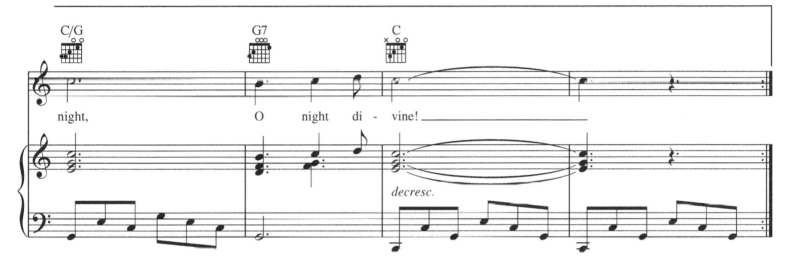

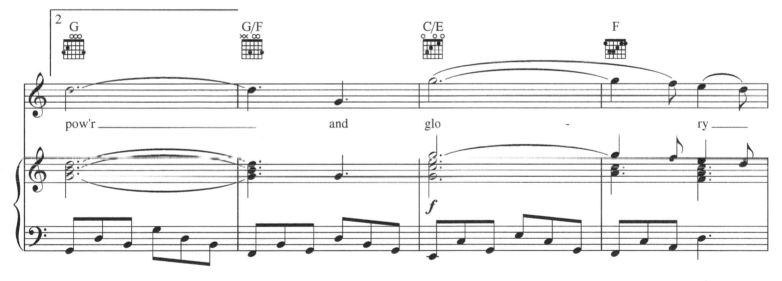

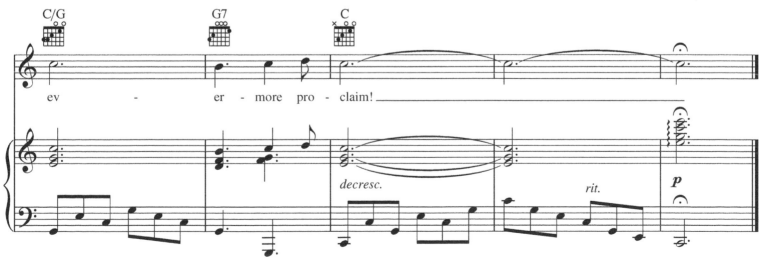

O LET US ALL BE GLAD TODAY

Words and Music by
MARTIN LUTHER

Slowly

1. O let us all be glad to-day, And
2. wake, my soul, from sad-ness rise. Come,
3.- 6. *(See additional verses)*

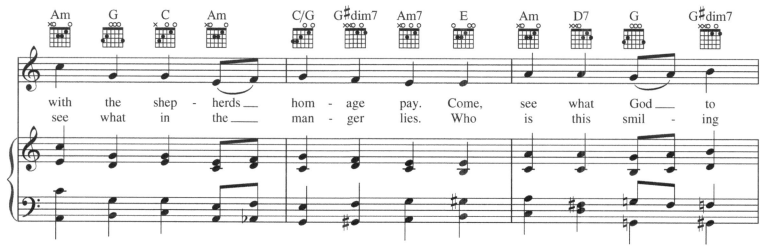

with the shep-herds hom-age pay. Come, see what God to
see what in the man-ger lies. Who is this smil-ing

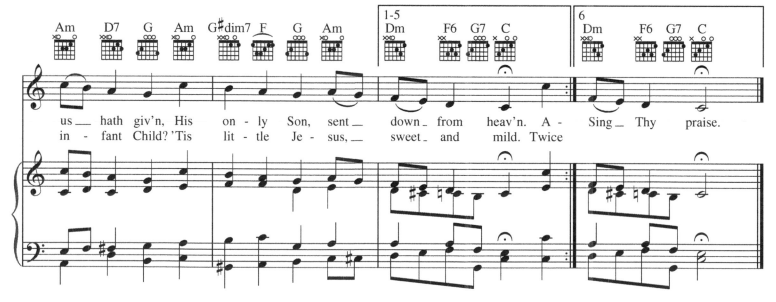

us hath giv'n, His on-ly Son, sent down from heav'n. A - Sing Thy praise.
in-fant Child? 'Tis lit-tle Je-sus, sweet and mild. Twice

Additional Verses

3. Twice welcome, O Thou heavenly guest,
   To save a world with sin distressed;
   Com'st Thou in lowly guise for me?
   What homage shall I give to Thee?

4. Ah! Lord eternal, heavenly King,
   Hast Thou become so mean a thing?
   And hast Thou left Thy blissful seat,
   To rest where colts and oxen eat?

5. Jesus, my Savior, come to me,
   Make here a little crib for Thee;
   A bed make in this heart of mine,
   That I may ay remember Thine.

6. Then from my soul glad songs shall ring;
   Of Thee each day I'll gladly sing;
   Then glad hosannas will I raise,
   From heart that loves to sing Thy praise.

RISE UP, SHEPHERD, AND FOLLOW

African-American Spiritual

fol - low. _____ Leave your ewes and leave your lambs.

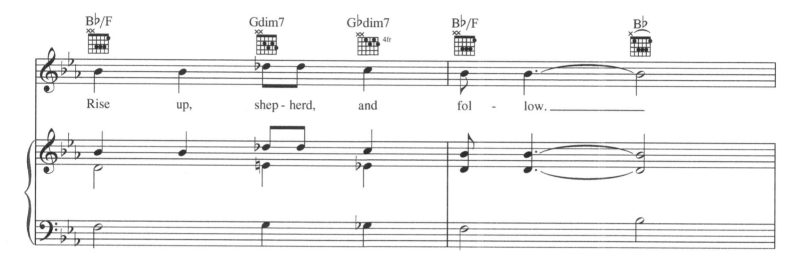

Rise up, shep - herd, and fol - low. _____

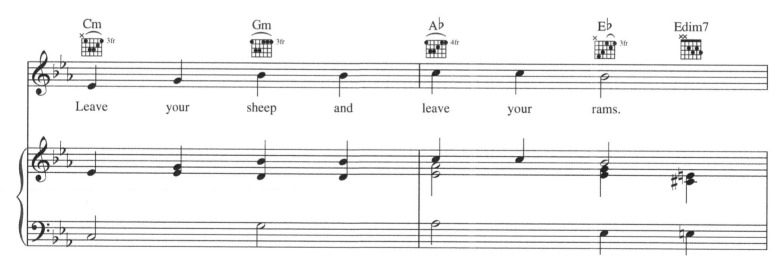

Leave your sheep and leave your rams.

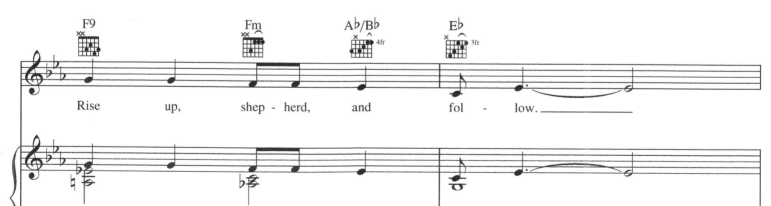

Rise up, shep - herd, and fol - low. _____

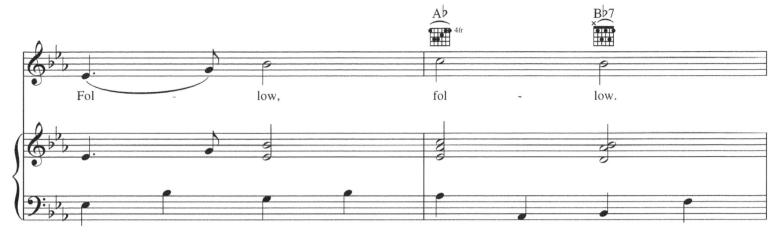

Fol - low, fol - low.

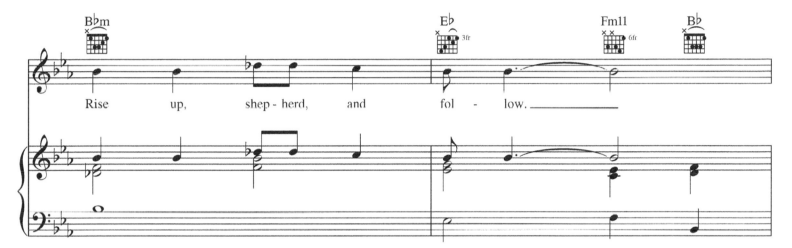

Rise up, shep - herd, and fol - low. _____

Fol - low the star of Beth - le - hem. _____

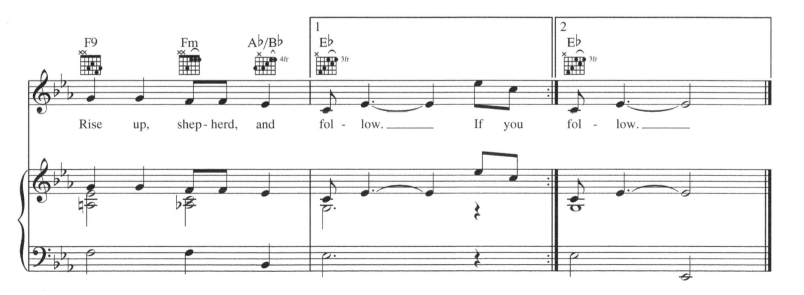

Rise up, shep - herd, and fol - low. _____ If you fol - low. _____

O LITTLE TOWN OF BETHLEHEM

Words by PHILLIPS BROOKS
Music by LEWIS H. REDNER

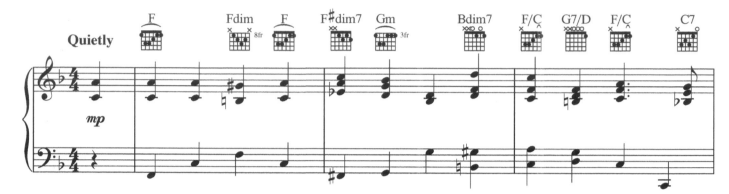

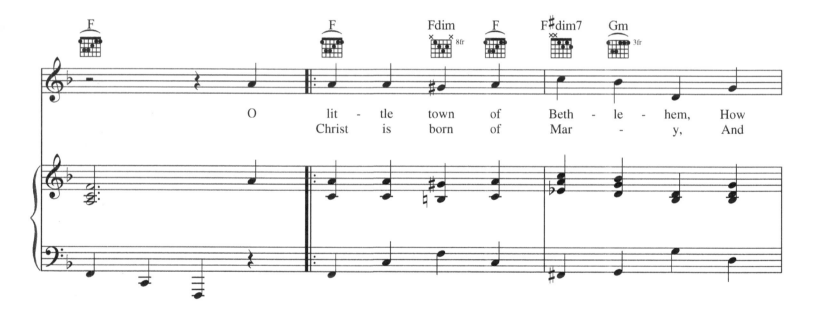

O lit - tle town of Beth - le - hem, How
Christ is born of Mar - y, And

still we ___ see thee lie! A - bove thy deep and
gath - ered ___ all a - bove, While mor - tals sleep and the

O SANCTISSIMA

Sicilian Carol

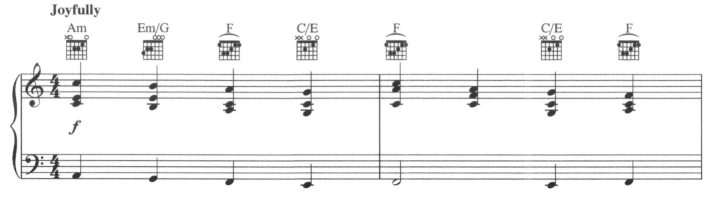

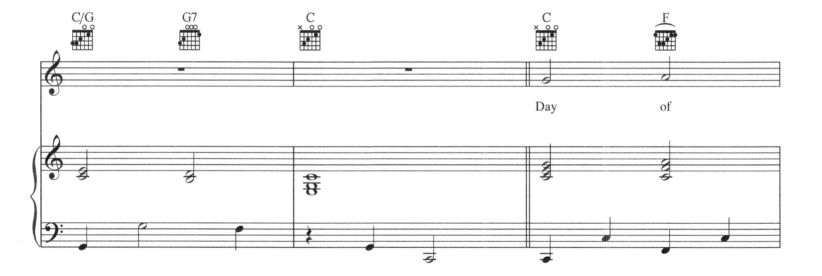

Day of

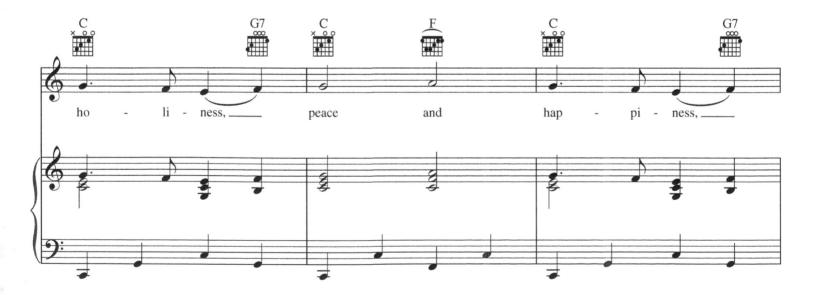

ho - li - ness, _____ peace and hap - pi - ness, _____

OF THE FATHER'S LOVE BEGOTTEN

Words by AURELIUS C. PRUDENTIUS
Translated by JOHN M. NEALE and HENRY W. BAKER
13th Century Plainsong

1. Of the Fa - ther's love be -
2. O that birth for - ev - er
3.-5. (See additional verses)

got - ten, Ere the worlds be - gan ___ to be,
bless - ed, When the vir - gin, full ___ of grace,

He is Al - pha and O - me - ga, He the Source, the End - ing
By the Ho - ly Ghost con - ceiv - ing, Bore the Sav - ior of our

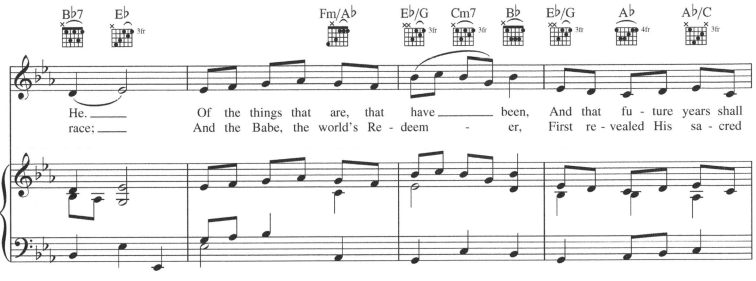

He. _____ Of the things that are, that have _____ been, And that fu - ture years shall
race; _____ And the Babe, the world's Re - deem - er, First re - vealed His sa - cred

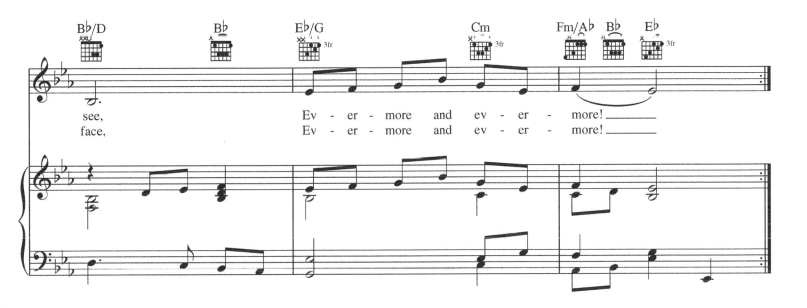

see, Ev - er - more and ev - er - more! _____
face, Ev - er - more and ev - er - more! _____

Additional Verses

3. This is He whom seers in old time
   Chanted of with one accord,
   Whom the voices of the prophets
   Promised in their faithful word.
   Now He shines, the long-expected;
   Let creation praise its Lord
   Evermore and evermore!

4. Let the heights of heav'n adore Him;
   Angel hosts, His praises sing.
   Pow'rs, dominions, bow before Him
   And extol our God and King.
   Let no tongue on earth be silent;
   Ev'ry voice in concert ring
   Evermore and evermore!

5. Christ, to Thee, with God the Father,
   And, O Holy Ghost, to Thee,
   Hymn and chant and high thanksgiving
   And unwearied praises be:
   Honor, glory and dominion
   And eternal victory
   Evermore and evermore!

ON CHRISTMAS NIGHT

Sussex Carol

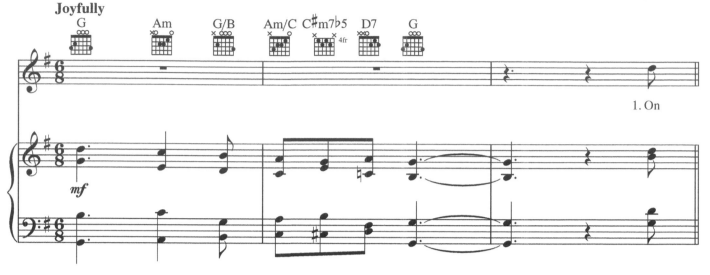

1. On

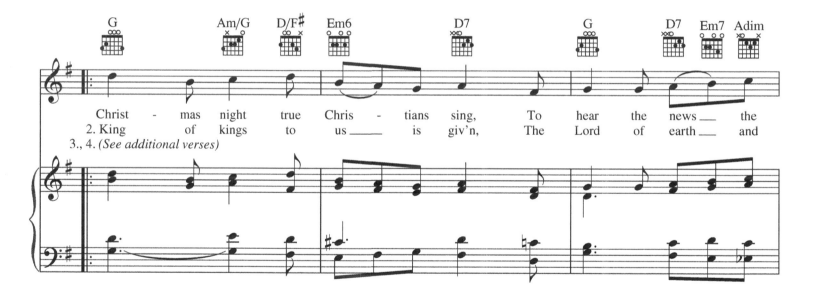

Christ - mas night true Chris - tians sing, To hear the news the
2. King of kings to us is giv'n, The Lord of earth and
3., 4. *(See additional verses)*

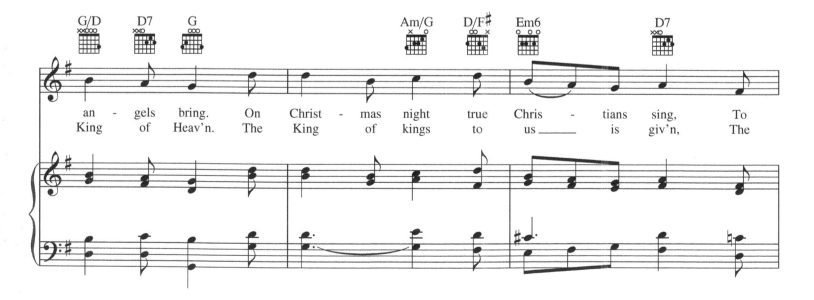

an - gels bring. On Christ - mas night true Chris - tians sing, To
King of Heav'n. The King of kings to us is giv'n, The

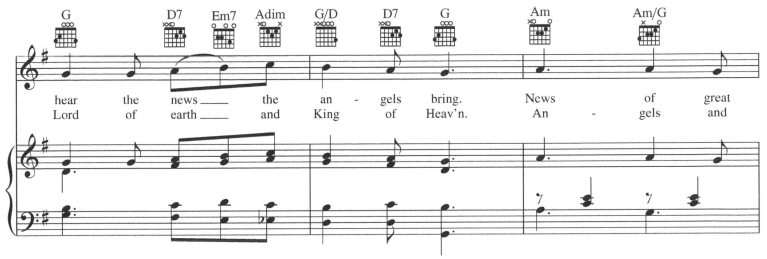

hear the news ___ the an - gels bring. News of great
Lord of earth ___ and King of Heav'n. An - gels great and

joy ___ and of ___ great mirth, Tid - ings
men ___ with joy ___ may sing Of blest

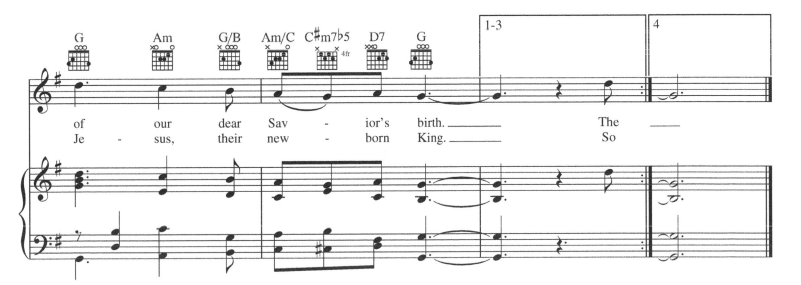

of our dear Sav - ior's birth. ___ The ___
Je - sus, their new - born King. ___ So

Additional Verses

3. So how on earth can men be sad,
   When Jesus comes to make us glad?
   So how on earth can men be sad,
   When Jesus comes to make us glad?
   From all our sins to set us free,
   Buying for us our liberty.

4. From out the darkness have we light,
   Which makes the angels sing this night.
   From out the darkness have we light,
   Which makes the angels sing this night:
   "Glory to God, His peace to men,
   And good will, evermore! Amen."

ONCE IN ROYAL DAVID'S CITY

Words by CECIL F. ALEXANDER
Music by HENRY J. GAUNTLETT

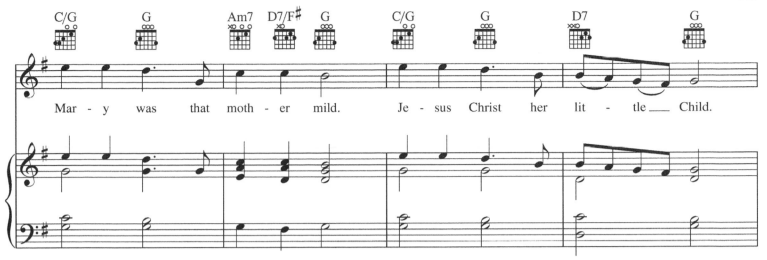

Mar - y was that moth - er mild. Je - sus Christ her lit - tle ___ Child.

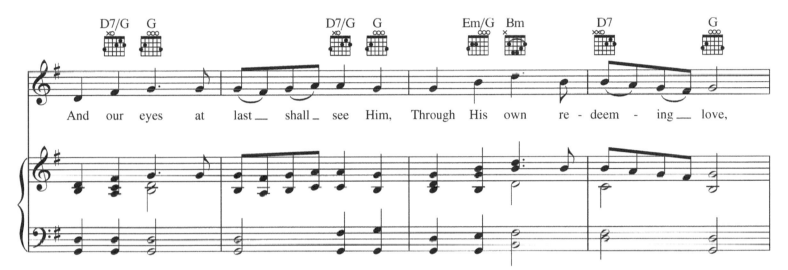

And our eyes at last ___ shall ___ see Him, Through His own re - deem - ing ___ love,

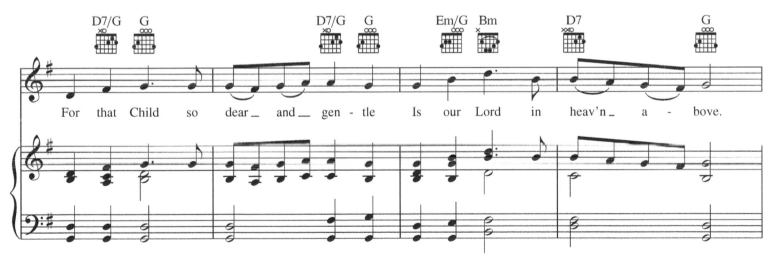

For that Child so dear ___ and ___ gen - tle Is our Lord in heav'n ___ a - bove.

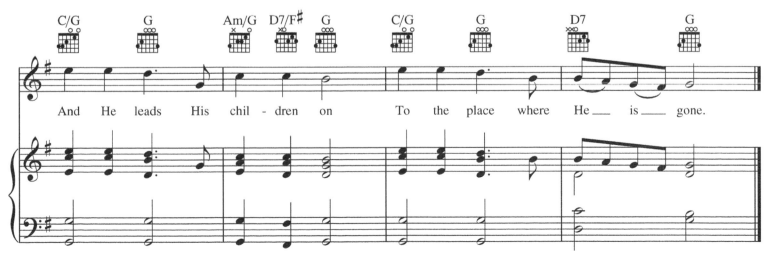

And He leads His chil - dren on To the place where He ___ is ___ gone.

PAT-A-PAN
(Willie, Take Your Little Drum)

Words and Music by
BERNARD de la MONNOYE

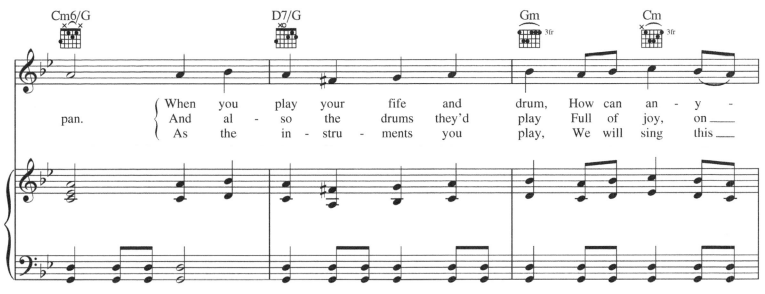

pan.

{ When you play your fife and drum, How can an - y -
And al - so the drums they'd play Full of joy, on ___
As the in - stru - ments you play, We will sing this ___

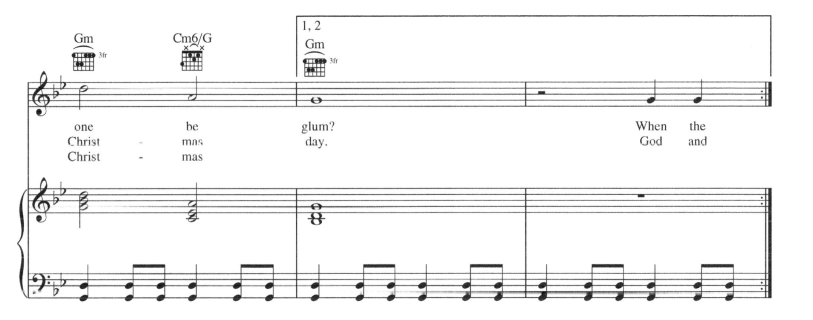

one be glum? When the
Christ - mas day. God and
Christ - mas

1, 2

3

day.

REJOICE AND BE MERRY

Gallery Carol

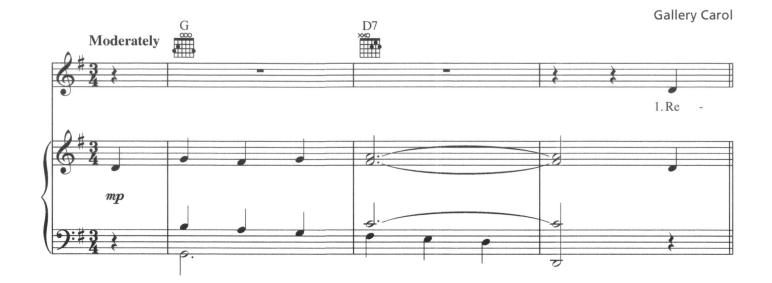

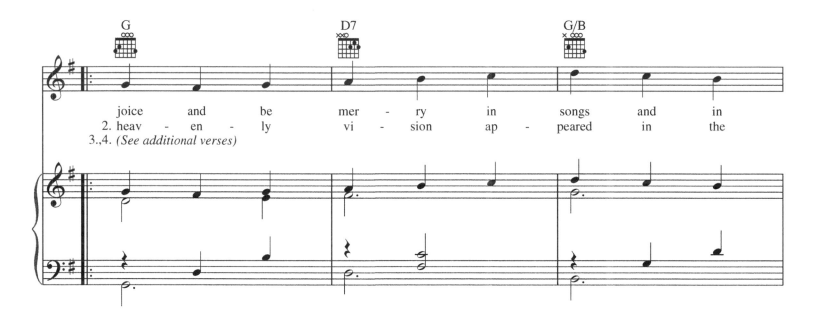

joice and be mer - ry in songs and in
2. heav - en - ly vi - sion ap - peared and in the
3.,4. (See additional verses)

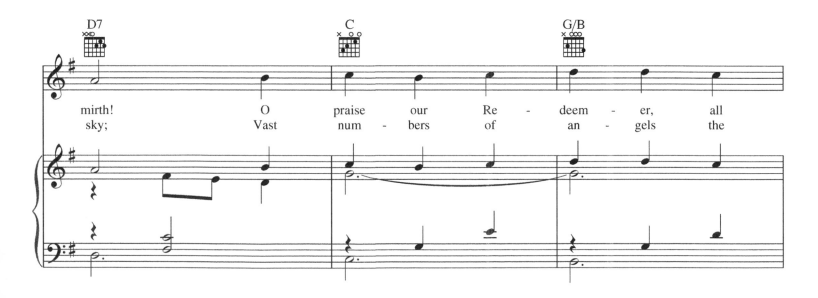

mirth! O praise our Re - deem - er, all
sky; Vast num - bers of an - gels all the

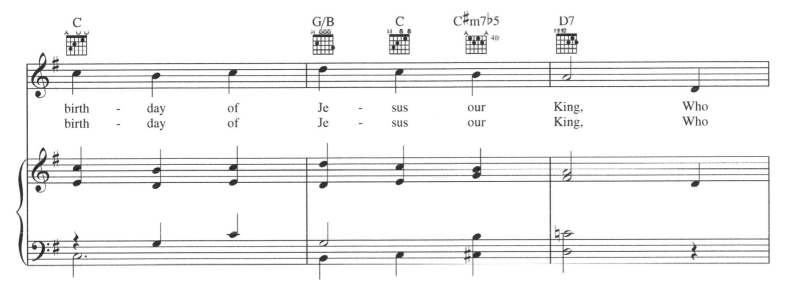

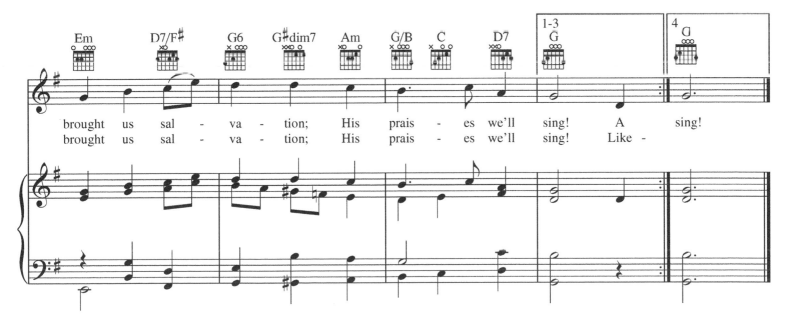

Additional Verses

3. Likewise a bright star in the sky did appear,
   Which led the wise men from the east to draw near.
   They found the Messiah, sweet Jesus our King,
   Who brought us salvation; His praises we'll sing!

4. And when they were come, they their treasures unfold,
   And unto Him offered myrrh, incense, and gold.
   So blessed forever be Jesus our King,
   Who brought us salvation; His praises we'll sing!

RING OUT, YE WILD AND MERRY BELLS

Words and Music by
C. MAITLAND

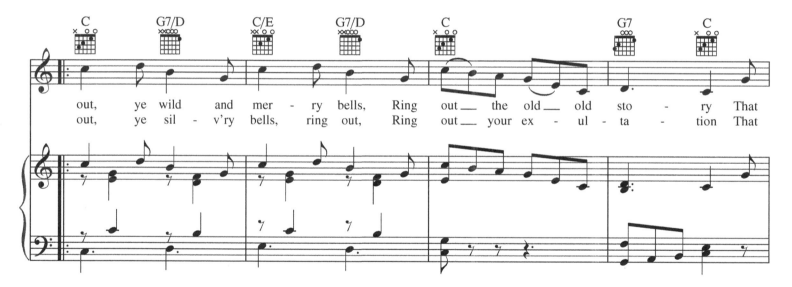

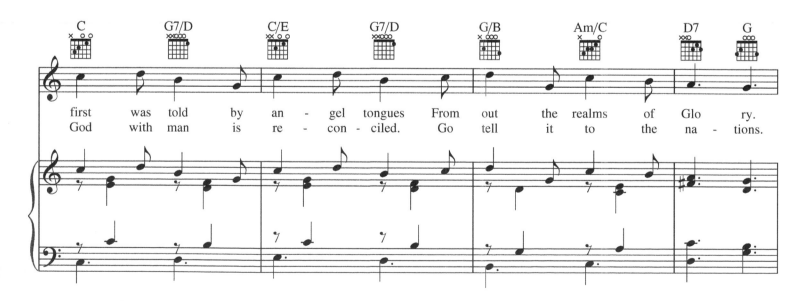

149

SHEPHERD! SHAKE OFF YOUR DROWSY SLEEP

Traditional French Carol

Shep - herd! shake off your drows - y sleep;
flow'rs all burst a - new, Rise and
up and quick a - way! Seek the

Think - ing

leave your sil - ly sheep.
snow is sum - mer dew.
Babe ere break of day.

An - gels from
See how from the
He is the

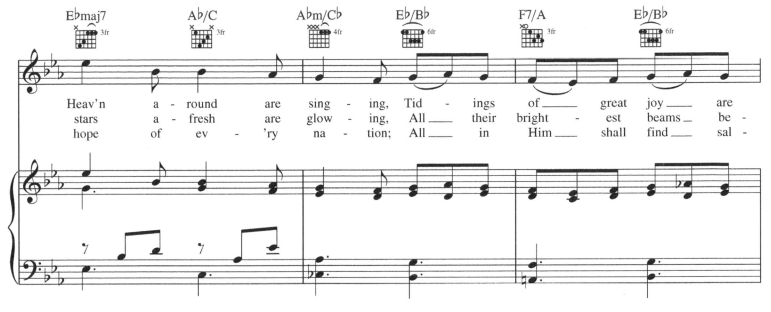

Heav'n a - round are sing - ing, Tid - ings of ____ great joy ____ are
stars a - fresh are glow - ing, All ____ their bright - est beams ____ be -
hope of ev - 'ry na - tion; All ____ in Him ____ shall find ____ sal -

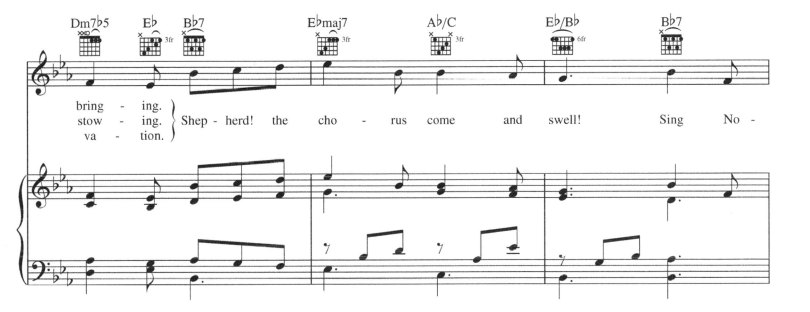

bring - ing. } Shep - herd! the cho - rus come and swell! Sing No -
stow - ing.
va - tion.

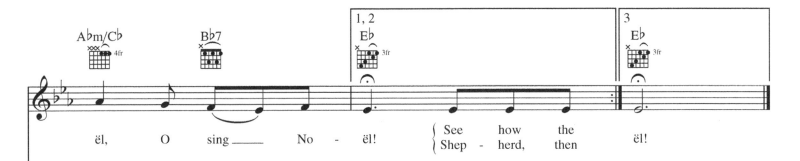

ël, O sing ____ No - ël! { See how the ël!
rit.   { Shep - herd, then

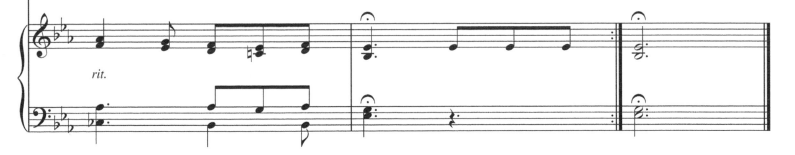

SHEPHERD'S CRADLE SONG

Words and Music by
C.D. SCHUBERT

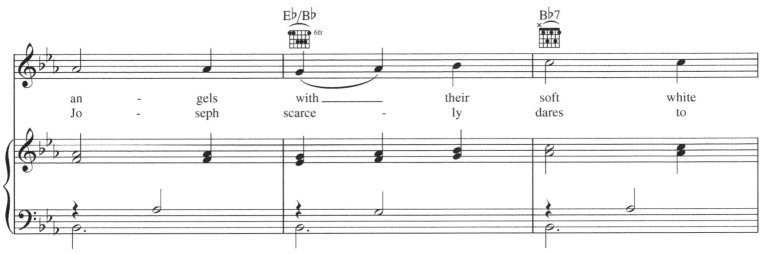

an - gels with _____ their soft white
Jo - seph scarce - ly dares to

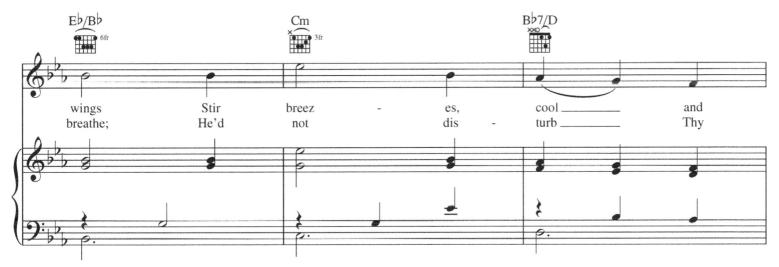

wings Stir breez - es, cool _____ and
breathe; He'd not dis - turb _____ Thy

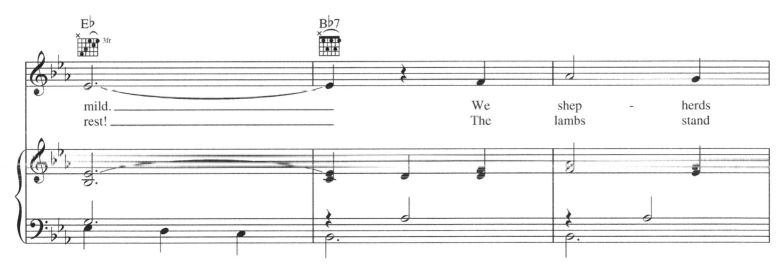

mild. _____ We shep - herds
rest! _____ The lambs stand

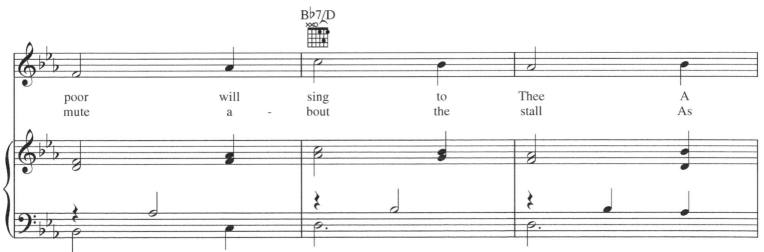

poor will sing to Thee A
mute a - bout the stall As

SING WE NOW OF CHRISTMAS

Traditional

Sing we now of Christ - mas, No - ël ___ sing we here. Sing our grate - ful prais - es To the ___ maid so dear.

Sing we No - ël! The King is born. No -

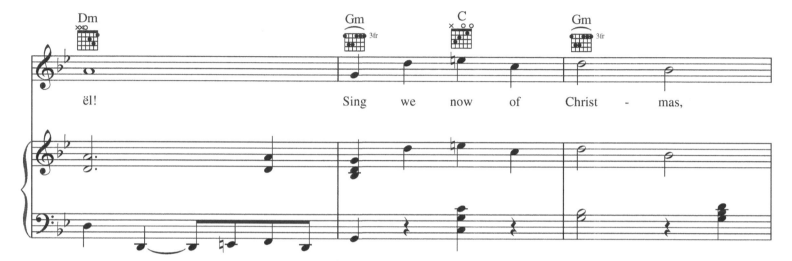

ël! Sing we now of Christ - mas,

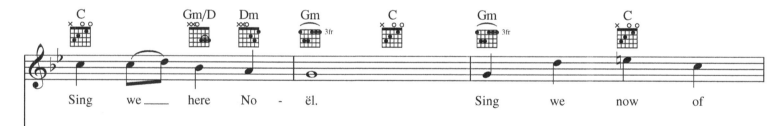

Sing we____ here No - ël. Sing we now of

Christ - mas, No - ël____ sing we here.

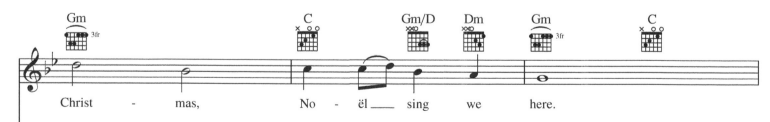

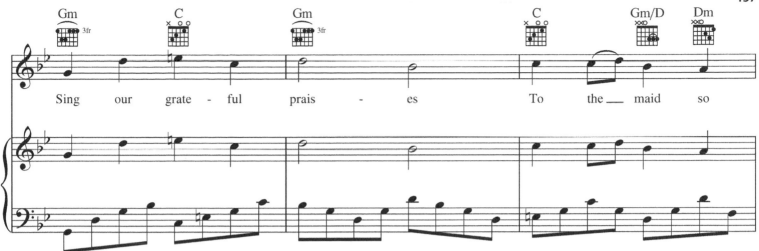

Sing our grate - ful prais - es To the __ maid so

dear. Sing we No - ël! The

King is born. No - ël! Sing we now of

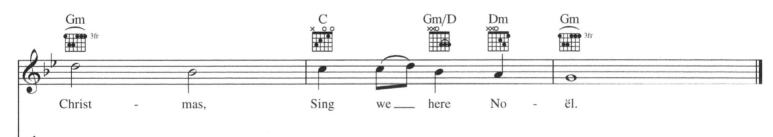

Christ - mas, Sing we __ here No - ël.

SHOUT THE GLAD TIDINGS

Traditional

D.S. al Fine

SILENT NIGHT

Words by JOSEPH MOHR
Translated by JOHN F. YOUNG
Music by FRANZ X. GRUBER

THE SIMPLE BIRTH

Traditional Flemish Carol

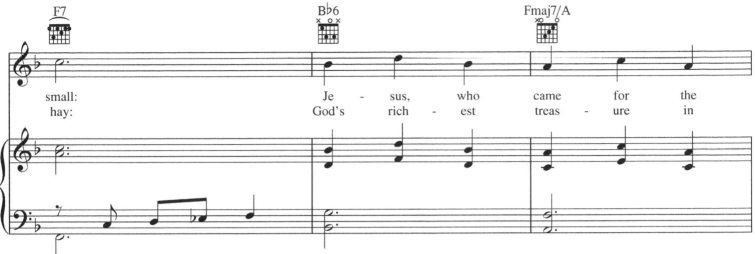

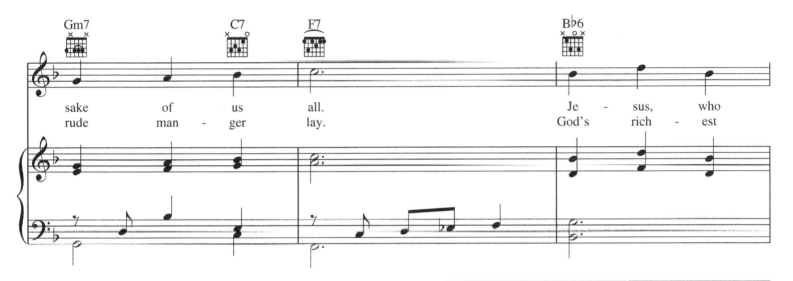

Additional Verses

3. His eyes of blackest jet were sparkling with light, *(Repeat)*
   Rosy cheeks bloomed on His face fair and bright. *(Repeat)*

4. And from His lovely mouth, the laughter did swell, *(Repeat)*
   When He saw Mary, whom He loved so well. *(Repeat)*

5. He came to weary earth, so dark and so drear, *(Repeat)*
   To wish mankind a blessed New Year. *(Repeat)*

SING, O SING, THIS BLESSED MORN

Words by CHRISTOPHER WORDSWORTH
Traditional German Tune

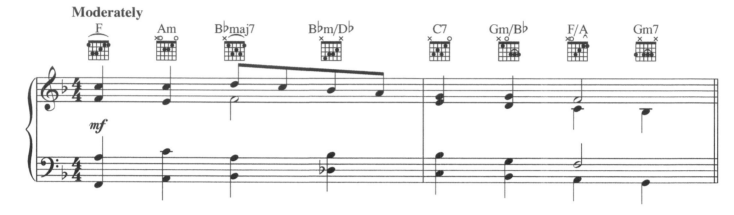

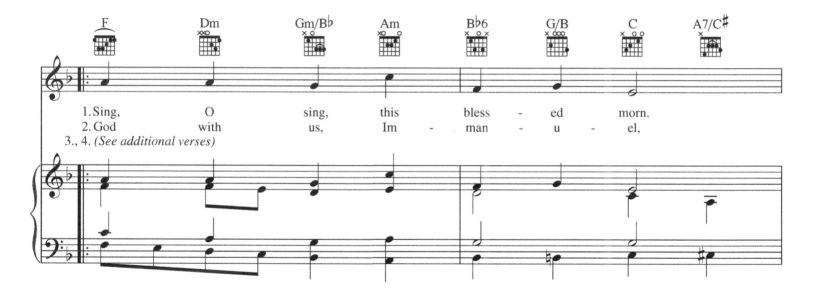

1. Sing, O sing, this bless - ed morn.
2. God with us, Im - man - u - el,
3., 4. *(See additional verses)*

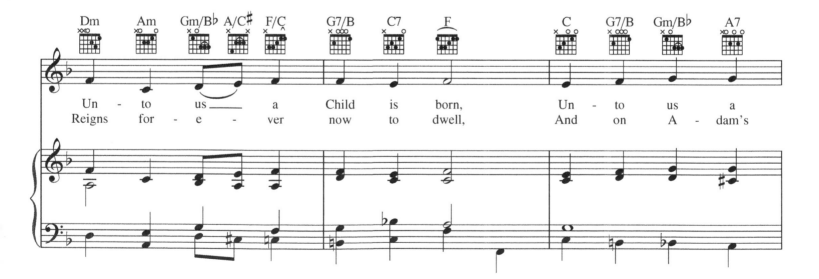

Un - to us ___ a Child is born, Un - to us a
Reigns for - e - ver now to dwell, And on A - dam's

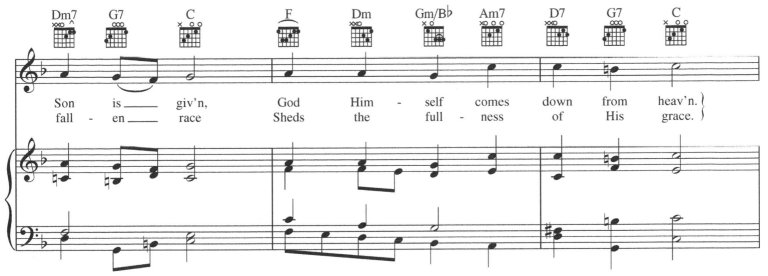

Son is_____ giv'n, God Him - self comes down from heav'n.
fall - en_____ race Sheds Him the self full - ness of His grace.

Refrain

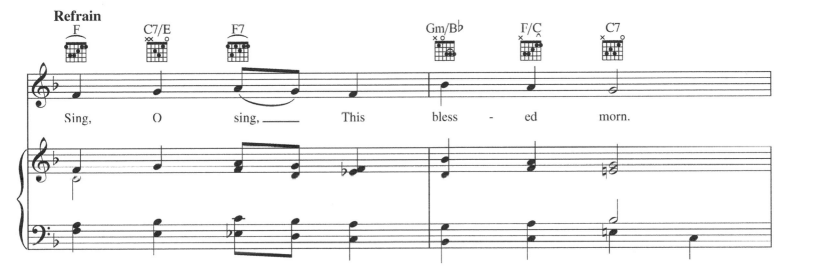

Sing, O sing, _____ This bless - ed morn.

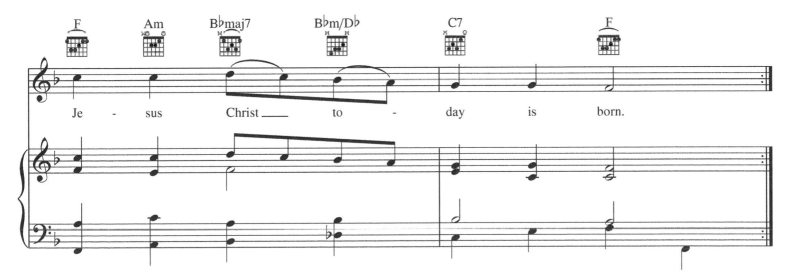

Je - sus Christ _____ to - day is born.

Additional Verses

3. God comes down that man may rise,
   Lifted by Him to the skies;
   Christ is Son of Man that we
   Son of God in Him may be:
   Refrain

4. O renew us, Lord, we pray,
   With Thy spirit day by day;
   That we ever one may be
   With the Father and with Thee:
   Refrain

SLEEP, HOLY BABE

Words by EDWARD CASWELL
Music by J.B. DYKES

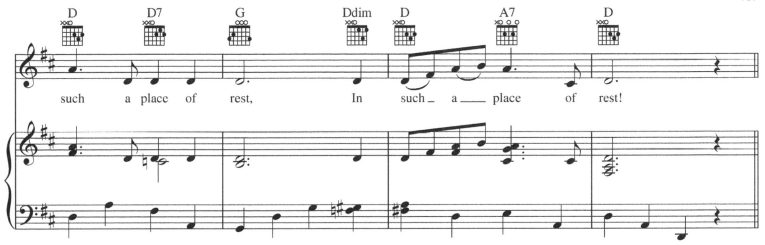

such a place of rest, In such a place of rest!

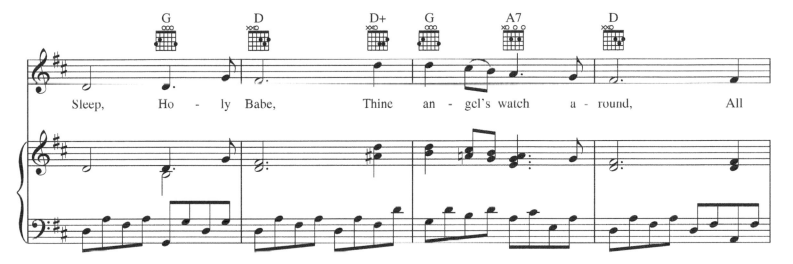

Sleep, Ho - ly Babe, Thine an - gel's watch a - round, All

bend - ing low with fold - ed wings Be - fore th'in - car - nate King of kings In

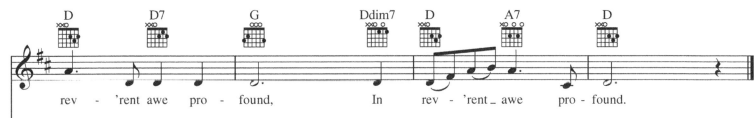

rev - 'rent awe pro - found, In rev - 'rent awe pro - found.

SLEEP, O SLEEP, MY PRECIOUS CHILD

Traditional Italian Carol

THE SNOW LAY ON THE GROUND

Traditional Irish Carol

THE STAR OF CHRISTMAS MORNING

Traditional

STAR OF THE EAST

Words by GEORGE COOPER
Music by AMANDA KENNEDY

Star of the east, O Beth-le-hem's star,
Star of the east, un-dimmed by each cloud,

Guid-ing us on to heav-en a-far.
What tho' the storms of grief gath-er loud?

Sor-row and grief are lulled by thy light, Thou
Faith-ful and pure, thy rays beam to save, Still

TOYLAND
from BABES IN TOYLAND

Words by GLEN MacDONOUGH
Music by VICTOR HERBERT

STILL, STILL, STILL

Salzburg Melody c. 1819
Traditional Austrian Text

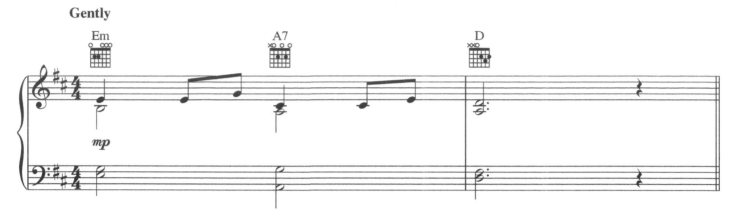

Still, _____ still, _____ still; to _____ sleep is _____ now His _____
Sleep, _____ sleep, _____ sleep, while _____ we Thy _____ vig - il _____

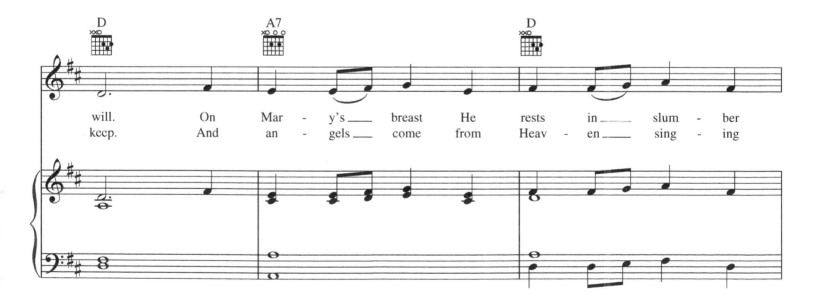

will. On Mar - y's _____ breast He rests in _____ slum - ber
keep. And an - gels _____ come from Heav - en _____ sing - ing

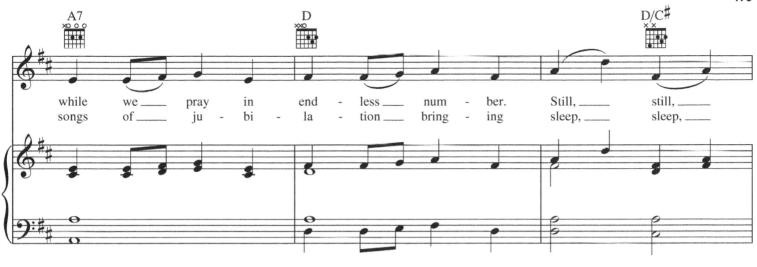

while we ___ pray in end - less ___ num - ber. Still, ___ still, ___
songs of ___ ju - bi - la - tion bring - ing sleep, ___ sleep, ___

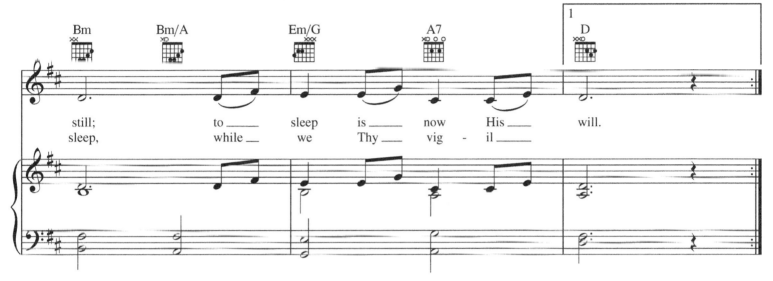

still; to ___ sleep is ___ now His ___ will.
sleep, while ___ we Thy ___ vig - il ___

keep. Sleep, ___ sleep, ___ sleep, ___ while ___

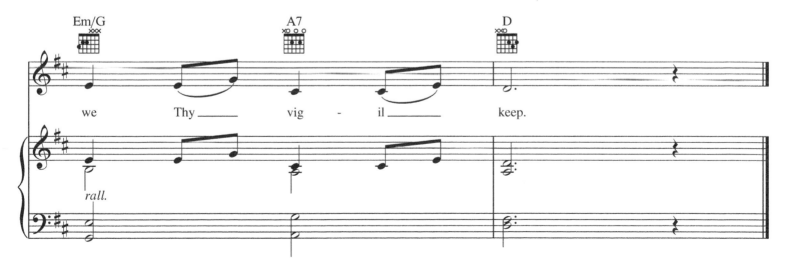

we Thy ___ vig - il ___ keep.

THERE'S A SONG IN THE AIR

Words and Music by JOSIAH G. HOLLAND
and KARL P. HARRINGTON

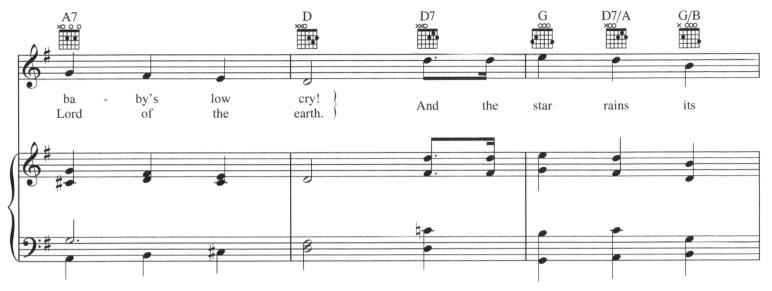

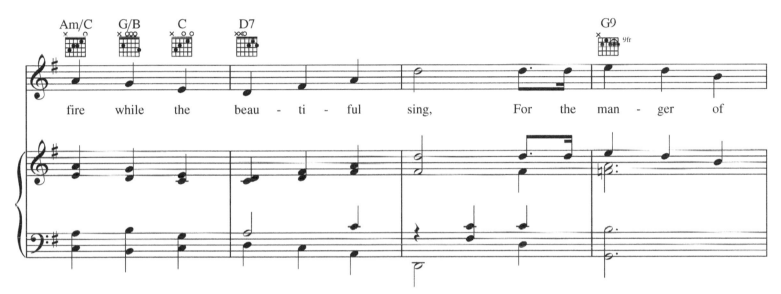

Additional Verses

3. In the light of that star
   Lie the ages impearled,
   And that song from afar
   Has swept over the world.
   Ev'ry hearth is aflame, and the angels sing
   In the homes of the nations that Jesus is King!

4. We rejoice in the light,
   And we echo the song
   That comes down thro' the night
   From the heavenly throng.
   Ay! we shout to the lovely evangel they bring
   And we greet in His cradle our Savior and King!

'TWAS THE NIGHT BEFORE CHRISTMAS

Words by CLEMENT CLARK MOORE
Music by F. HENRI KLICKMAN

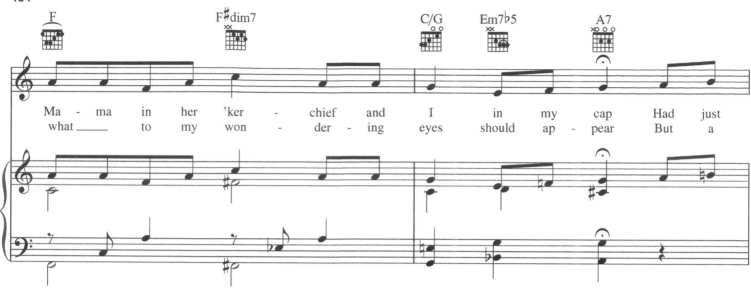

Additional Verses

3. With a little old driver so lively and quick,
I knew in a moment it must be St. Nick.
More rapid than eagles his coursers they came,
And he whistled, and shouted, and called them by name:
"Now, Dasher! Now, Dancer! Now, Prancer! Now Vixen!
On, Comet! On, Cupid, On Donder and Blitzen!
To the top of the porch, to the top of the wall!
Now dash away, dash away, dash away all!"

4. As dry leaves that before the wild hurricane fly,
When they meet with an obstacle, mount to the sky,
So up to the house-top the coursers they flew,
With the sleigh full of toys, and St. Nicholas, too.
And then in a twinkling I heard on the roof
The prancing and pawing of each little hoof.
As I drew in my head, and was turning around,
Down the chimney St. Nicholas came with a bound.

5. He was dressed all in fur from his head to his foot,
And his clothes were all tarnished with ashes and soot;
A bundle of toys he had flung on his back,
And he looked like a peddler just opening his pack.
His eyes how they twinkled! His dimples how merry!
His cheeks were like roses, his nose like a cherry.
His droll little mouth was drawn up like a bow,
And the beard of his chin was as white as the snow.

6. The stump of a pipe he held tight in his teeth,
And the smoke, it encircled his head like a wreath.
He had a broad face, and a round little belly
That shook, when he laughed, like a bowl full of jelly.
He was chubby and plump, a right jolly old elf,
And I laughed when I saw him, in spite of myself.
A wink of his eye, and a twist of his head,
Soon gave me to know I had nothing to dread.

7. He spoke not a word, but went straight to his work,
And filled all the stockings; then turned with a jerk,
And laying his finger aside of his nose,
And giving a nod, up the chimney he rose.
He sprang to his sleigh, to his team gave a whistle,
And away they all fled like the down of a thistle;
But I heard him exclaim, ere he drove out of sight:
"Happy Christmas to all, and to all a Good-night!"

THE TWELVE DAYS OF CHRISTMAS

Traditional English Carol

On the first day of Christ-mas, my true love gave to me a par-tridge in a pear tree.

On the sec-ond day of Christ-mas, my true love sent to me:
third __ day of Christ-mas, my true love sent to me:
fourth __ day of Christ-mas, my true love sent to me:

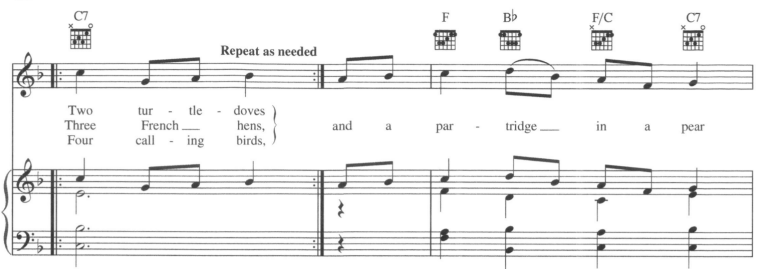

Two tur - tle - doves
Three French ___ hens,
Four call - ing birds, and a par - tridge ___ in a pear

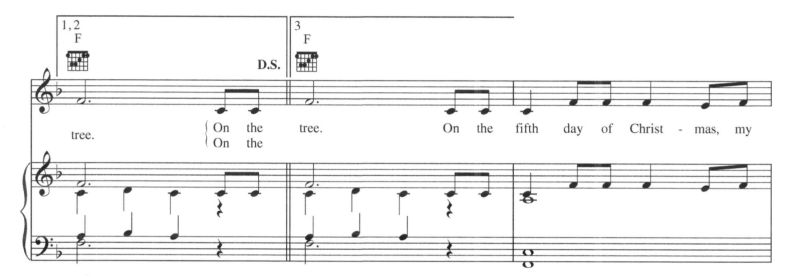

tree. On the tree. On the On the fifth day of Christ - mas, my

true love sent to me: Five gold _____ rings!

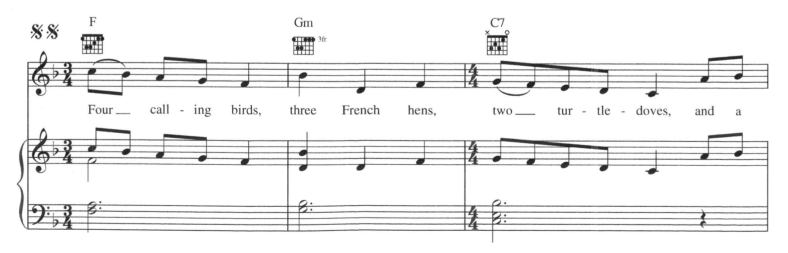

Four ___ call - ing birds, three French hens, two ___ tur - tle - doves, and a

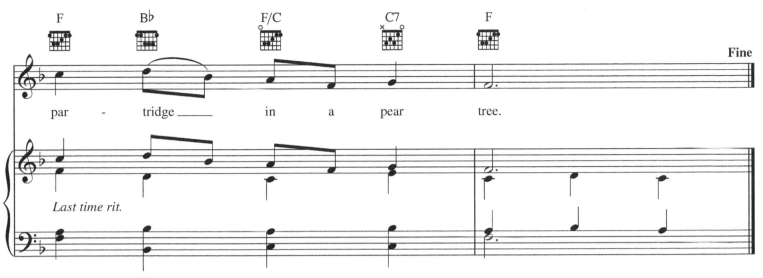

A VIRGIN UNSPOTTED

Traditional English Carol

1. A virgin unspotted, the prophet foretold,
2. God sent an angel from Heaven so high,
3., 4. (See additional verses)

told, Should bring forth a Savior, which we now behold;
high, To certain poor shepherds in fields where they

hold; To be our Redeemer from death, hell and
lie, And bade them no longer in sorrow to

sin, Which Ad - am's trans - gres - sion had wrap - pcd us
stay, Be - cause that our Sav - ior was born on this

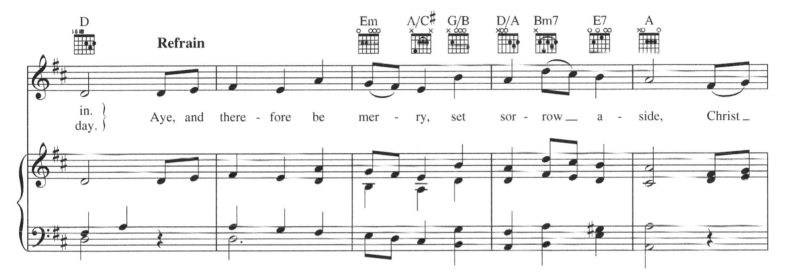

Refrain

in. } Aye, and there - fore be mer - ry, set sor - row a - side, Christ
day. }

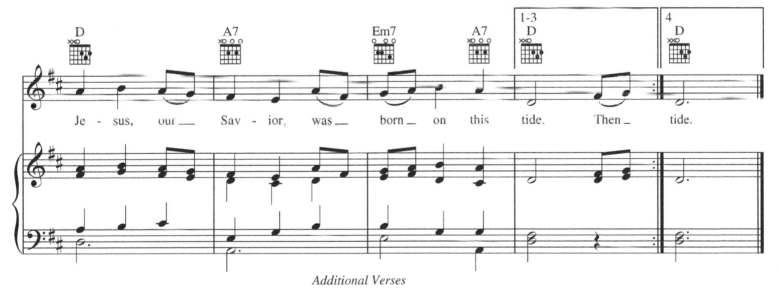

Je - sus, our Sav - ior, was born on this tide. Then tide.

Additional Verses

3. Then presently after, the shepherds did spy
   Vast numbers of angels to stand in the sky;
   They joyfully talked and sweetly did sing:
   "To God be all glory, our heavenly King."
   Refrain

4. To teach us humility all this was done,
   And learn we from thence haughty pride for to shun;
   A manger His cradle who came from above,
   The great God of mercy, of peace and of love.
   Refrain

WATCHMAN, TELL US OF THE NIGHT

Traditional

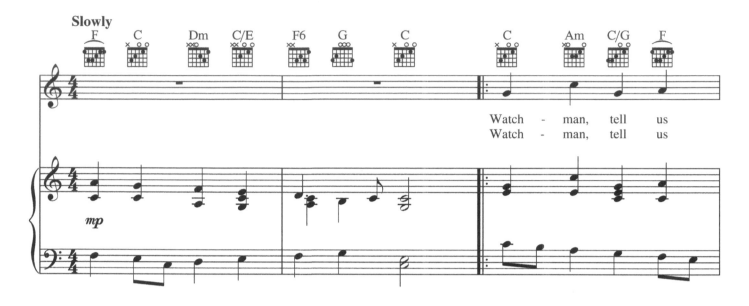

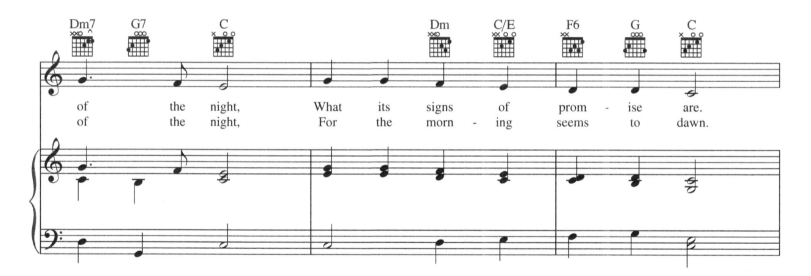

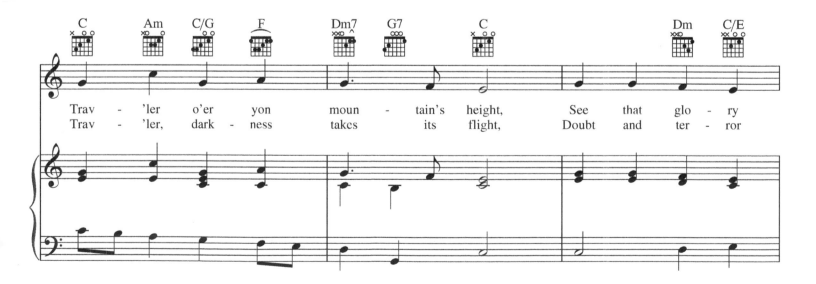

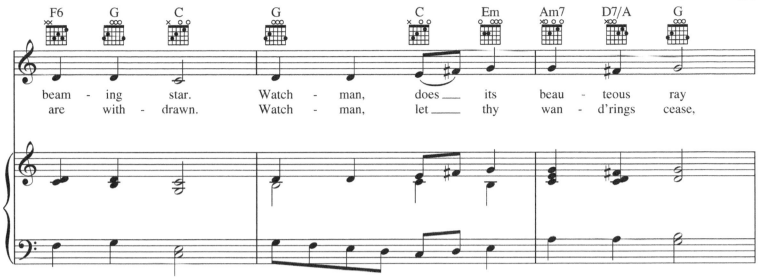

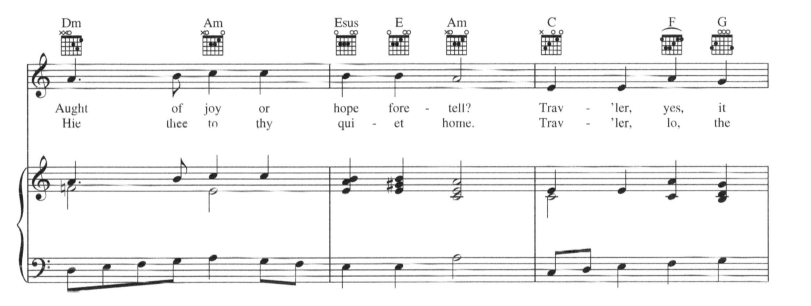

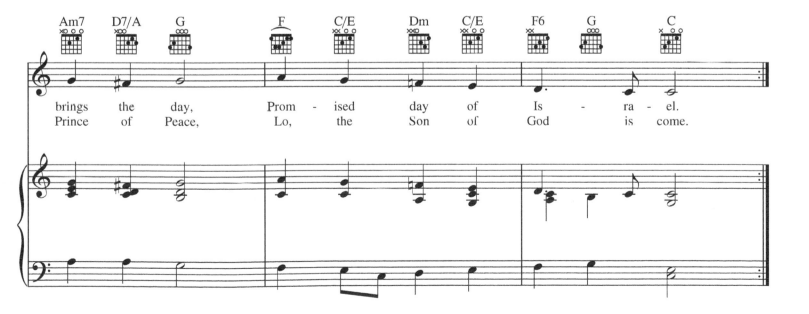

WE THREE KINGS OF ORIENT ARE

Words and Music by
JOHN H. HOPKINS, JR.

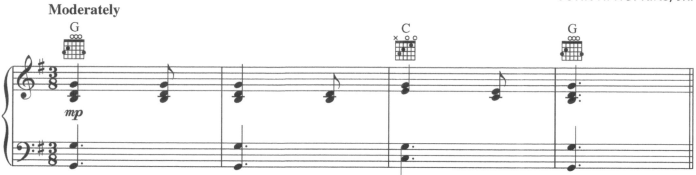

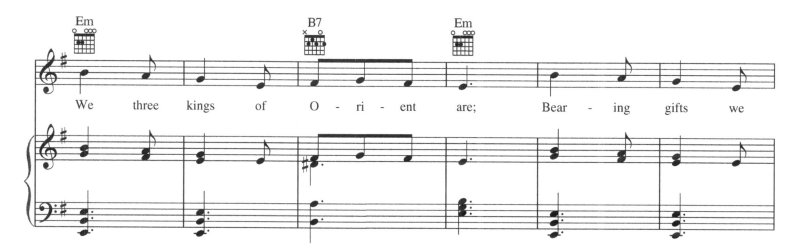

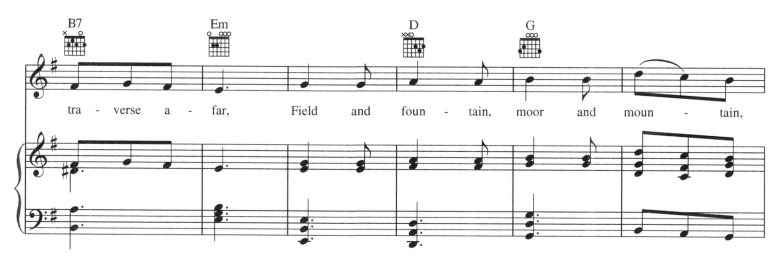

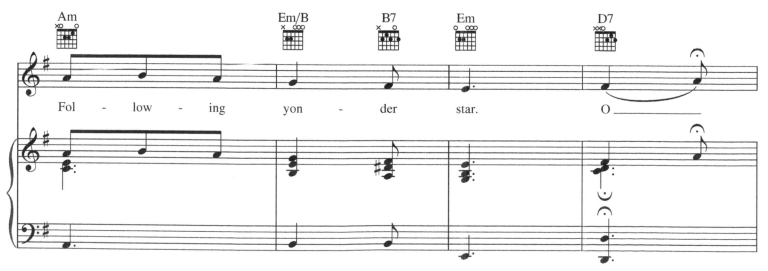

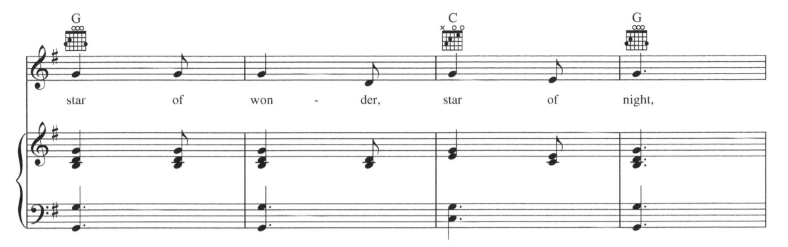

star of won - der, star of night,

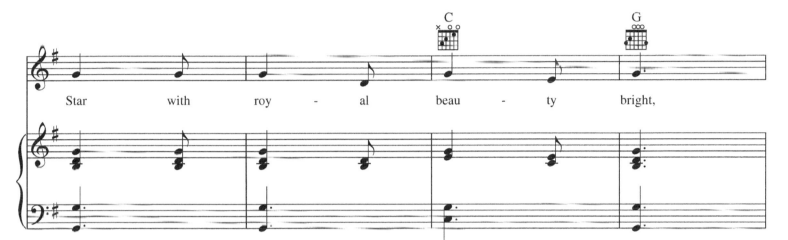

Star with roy - al beau - ty bright,

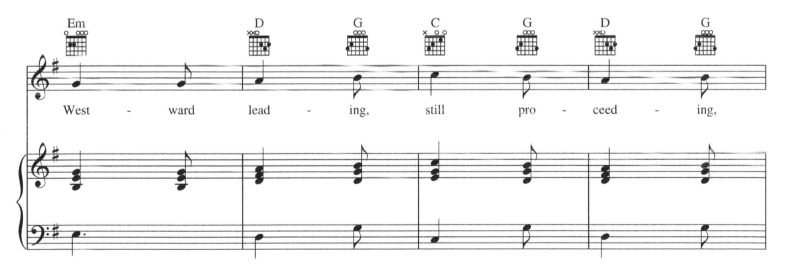

West - ward lead - ing, still pro - ceed - ing,

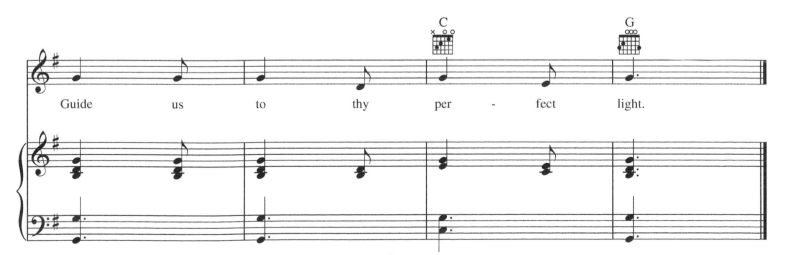

Guide us to thy per - fect light.

WE WISH YOU A MERRY CHRISTMAS

Traditional English Folksong

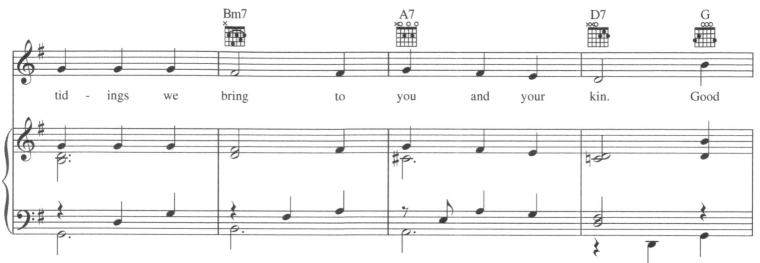

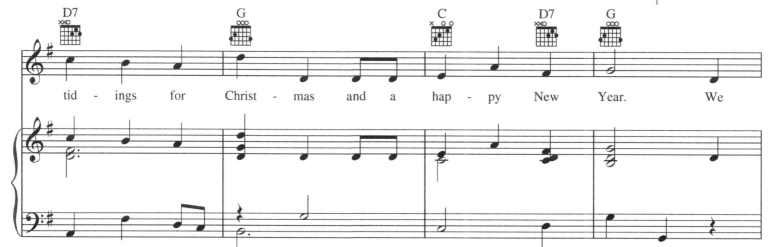

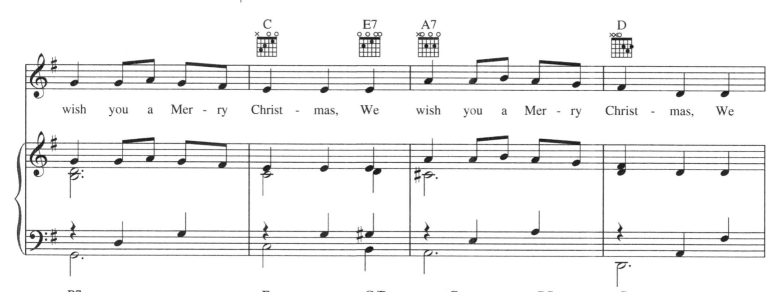

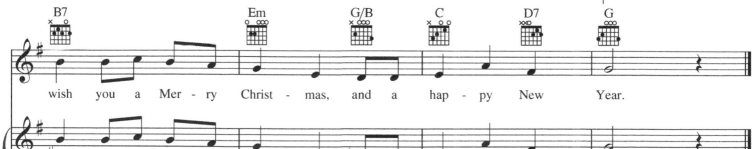

WHAT CHILD IS THIS?

Words by WILLIAM C. DIX
16th Century English Melody

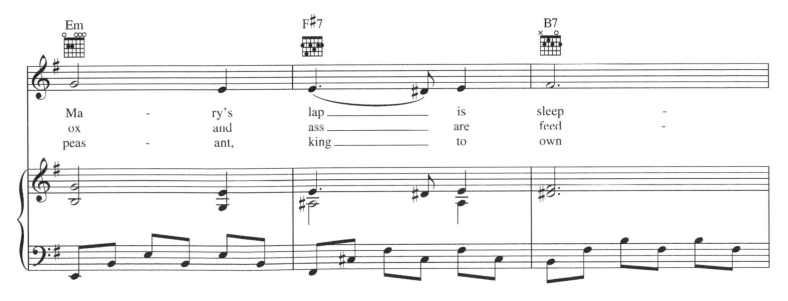

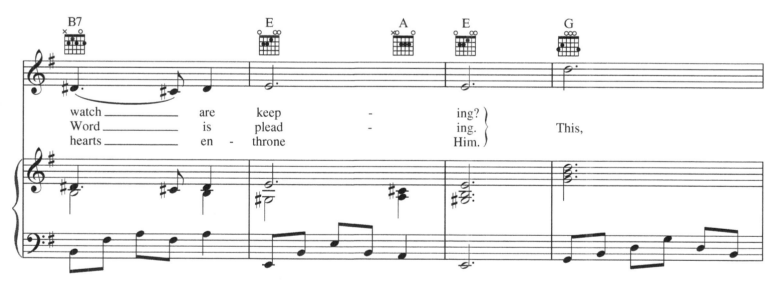

guard _____ and an - gels sing:

Haste, haste _____ to bring him

laud, _____ the babe, _____ the son _____ of

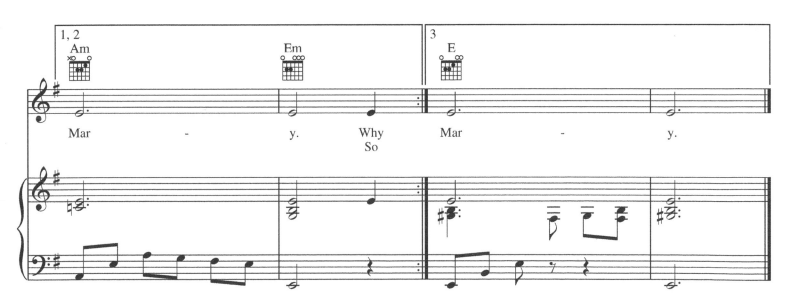

Mar - y. Why Mar - y.
So

WEXFORD CAROL

Traditional Irish Carol

1. Good peo - ple _ all this Christ - mas time, Con - sid - er well _ and
2. night be - fore that hap - py tide, The no - ble vir - gin
3.-5. *(See additional verses)*

bear in mind What our good _ God for us has done In send - ing His _ be -
and her guide Were long time _ seek - ing up and down To find a lodg - ing

Additional Verses

3. Near Bethlehem did shepherds keep
   Their flocks of lambs and feeding sheep;
   To whom God's angels did appear,
   Which put the shepherds in great fear.
   "Prepare and go," the angels said,
   "To Bethlehem, be not afraid;
   For there you'll find this happy morn
   A princely Babe, sweet Jesus born."

4. With thankful heart and joyful mind,
   The shepherds went, the Babe to find;
   And as God's angel had foretold,
   They did our Savior Christ behold.
   Within a manger He was laid,
   And by His side, the virgin maid,
   Attending on the Lord of life,
   Who came to earth to end all strife.

5. There were three wise men from afar,
   Directed by a glorious star;
   And on they wandered night and day,
   Until they came where Jesus lay.
   And when they came unto that place
   Where our beloved Messiah was,
   They humbly cast them at His feet,
   With gifts of gold and incense sweet.

WHEN CHRIST WAS BORN OF MARY FREE

Traditional English Carol

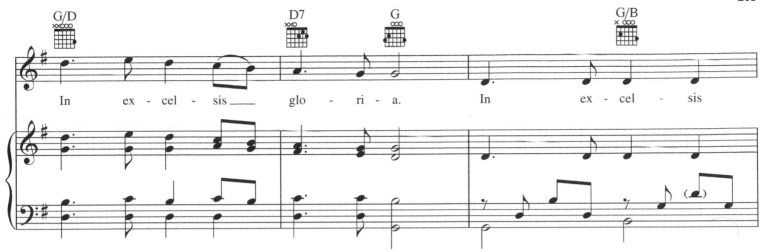

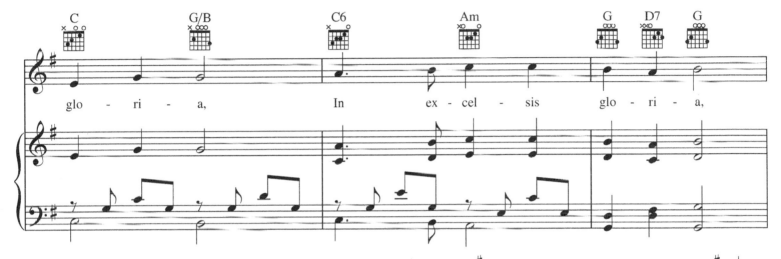

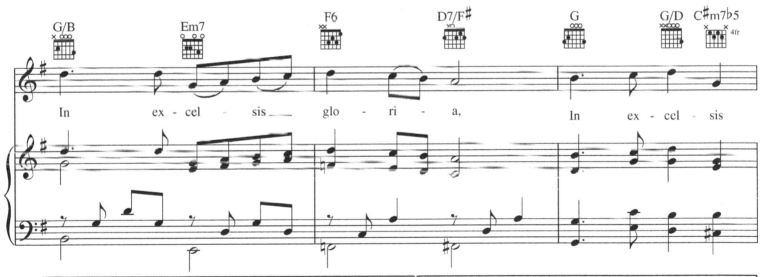

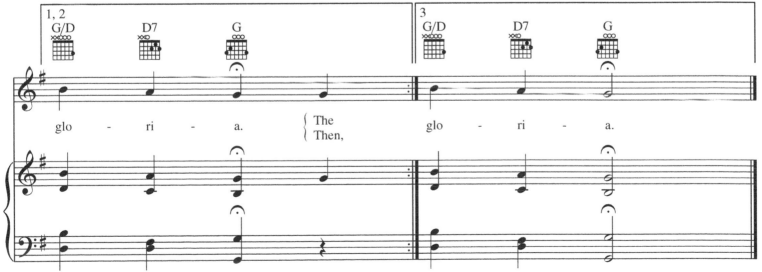

WHEN CHRISTMAS MORN
IS DAWNING

Traditional Swedish

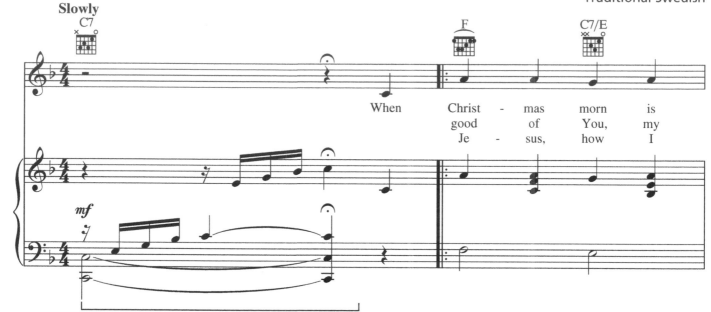

When Christ - mas morn is
good of You, my Je - sus, how I

dawn - ing, In hum - ble faith I'd
Sav - ior, To come heav - 'n dear - est
need Thee, The chil - dren's

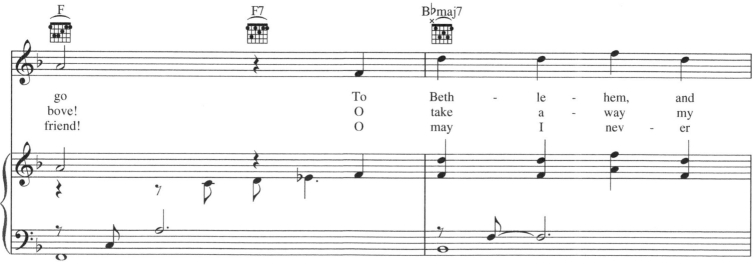

go bove! To Beth - le - hem, and
O take a - way my
friend! O may I nev - er

WHILE SHEPHERDS WATCHED THEIR FLOCKS BY NIGHT

Words by NAHUM TATE
Music by GEORGE FRIDERIC HANDEL

1. While shep-herds watched their flocks by night, All
2. not!" said he, for might-y dread Had
3.-6. (See additional verses)

seat-ed on the ground, The an-gel of the
seized their trou-bled mind, "Glad tid-ings of great

Lord came down, and glory shone a - round, And
joy I bring, To you and all man - kind, To

glo - ry shone a - round. "Fear cease!"
you and all man - kind. To

Additional Verses

3. To you, in David's town this day,
   Is born of David's line,
   The Savior, who is Christ the Lord;
   And this shall be the sign,
   And this shall be the sign:

4. The heavenly Babe you there shall find
   To human view displayed,
   All meanly wrapped in swathing bands,
   And in a manger laid,
   And in a manger laid."

5. Thus spake the seraph; and forthwith
   Appeared a shining throng
   Of angels praising God on high,
   Who thus addressed their song,
   Who thus addressed their song:

6. "All glory be to God on high,
   And to the earth be peace;
   Good will henceforth from heav'n to men,
   Begin and never cease,
   Begin and never cease!"

NDS THROUGH THE OLIVE TREES

19th Century American Carol

Tenderly

Winds through the ol - ive trees Soft - ly did blow
Sheep on the hill - side lay, Whit - er than snow,
Then from the hap - py skies, An - gels bent low,
For in a man - ger bed, Cra - dled we know,

'Round lit - tle Beth - le - hem, Long, long a - go.
Shep - herds were watch - ing them, Long, long a - go.
Sing - ing their songs of joy, Long, long a - go.
Christ came to Beth - le - hem, Long, long a - go.

Long, long a - go.